W9-AWS-023

Martin Luther and the Called Life

Martin Luther and the Called Life

Mark D. Tranvik

Fortress Press
Minneapolis

MARTIN LUTHER AND THE CALLED LIFE

Copyright © 2016 Fortress Press. All rights reserved. Except for brief
quotations in critical articles or reviews, no part of this book may be
reproduced in any manner without prior written permission from the
publisher.
Visit http://www.augsburgfortress.org/copyrights/ or write to
Permissions, Augsburg Fortress, Box 1209, Minneapolis, MN 55440.

Cover design: Alisha Lofgren

Library of Congress Cataloging-in-Publication Data
Print ISBN: 978-1-4514-9011-4
eBook ISBN: 978-1-5064-1038-8

The paper used in this publication meets the minimum requirements of
American National Standard for Information Sciences — Permanence of
Paper for Printed Library Materials, ANSI Z329.48-1984.

Manufactured in the U.S.A.

This book was produced using Pressbooks.com, and PDF rendering was
done by PrinceXML.

Contents

Acknowledgements

Many people made this book possible. I begin with my students at Augsburg College, where I have taught for the past twenty years. They have often heard about Martin Luther and vocation in my classes. They have responded with honest puzzlement, perceptive questions, and helpful clarifications. More than anything else, they have insisted that Luther's ideas be grounded in real life, which is a perfectly reasonable expectation for a book on vocation.

My calling in the world of work for the first ten years of my adult life was as a parish pastor. Those years at Cross of Glory Lutheran Church in Brooklyn Center, Minnesota, were formative in so many ways. In particular, I learned that most of the people in the pews really do yearn for ways to think about how to live a Christian life beyond the walls of a church building. In some ways, this book is a very belated response to that desire to carry faith into the home, workplace, and public square.

My colleagues at Augsburg have also made this book much stronger. I think, first of all, of my fellow teachers in the Religion Department: Lori Brandt Hale, Jeremy Myers, Phil Quanbeck II, Russell Kleckley, Bev Stratton, Marty Stortz, Brad

Holt, Hans Wiersma, Mary Lowe, David Tiede, and Matt Maruggi. Together, we have made vocation a central concept in our curriculum and that has resulted in many fascinating conversations in retreats, seminars, and hallways. A similar indebtedness is due to Diane Glorvigen, Jack Fortin, and Lonna Field, all of whom worked with me in the Christensen Center for Vocation. This book has also been supported by the administration of the college—in particular, the past and present presidents of Augsburg, Bill Frame and Paul Pribbenow. They have taught me much about the value of vocation when practiced by people responsible for guiding and leading institutions.

Others in the faith and academic communities have also offered counsel about various drafts of the text. In particular, I want to thank Ali Tranvik, Isak Tranvik (daughter-in-law and son, respectively), Paul McGlasson, Mark Mattes, and Jim Nestingen. A special word of thanks goes out to Robert Kolb, who commented on one of the later drafts, and, as usual, made some excellent observations. Thanks, too, to my editors at Fortress Press, Will Bergkamp and Scott Tunseth, for their patience and suggestions—the latter made the final draft considerably better. Finally, I must also add the usual caveat that none of the above is responsible for the book's flaws.

The book is dedicated to my wife, Ann, and our sons, Isak and David. They have taught me much about what it means to live out a calling as a spouse and father. In my relationship with each of them, down through the years, they have had many opportunities to exercise forgiveness and I am deeply grateful they have chosen to do so.

Abbreviations

BC   *The Book of Concord: The Confessions of the Evangelical Lutheran Church.* Ed. Robert Kolb and Timothy J. Wengert, trans. Charles Arand et al. Minneapolis: Fortress Press, 2000.

Brecht   Martin Brecht, *Martin Luther.* 3 vols. Trans. James L. Schaaf. Minneapolis: Fortress Press, 1985–93.

LW   Martin Luther, *Luther's Works.* American Edition. 55 vols. St. Louis and Philadelphia: Concordia and Fortress Press, 1958–86.

TR   Martin Luther, *D. Martin Luthers Werke: Kritische Gesamtausgabe, Tischreden.* 6 vols. Weimar: Hermann Böhlaus Nachfolger, 1912–21.

WA   Martin Luther, *D. Martin Luthers Werke: Kritische Gesamtausgaber.* 65 vols. In 127. H. Böhlaus, 1883–1993.

Martin Luther Timeline

1483	Born in Eisleben.
1505	Begins law studies and has experience in thunderstorm. Enters Augustinian monastery in Erfurt.
1507	Ordained a priest.
1512–13	Receives Doctor of Theology degree and begins teaching at the University of Wittenberg.
1517	Posts *The Ninety-five Theses*.
1518	*Heidelberg Disputation*.
1519	Leipzig Debate with John Eck.
1520	Writes *The Freedom of a Christian*.
1521	Excommunicated by the pope.
1521	Appears before the Diet of Worms and is declared an outlaw of the Holy Roman Empire.
1521–22	Confinement in Wartburg Castle. Translates New Testament into German.
1525	Peasants' War.
1525	Marriage to Katherine von Bora.
1529	Writes the *Small and Large Catechisms*.
1530	*Augsburg Confession* written by Luther's colleague, Philip Melanchthon.
1542	Death of daughter, Magdalene.
1546	Martin Luther dies in Eisleben.

Introduction

> Ask people the following: when they are on the job, walking or standing still, eating, drinking, sleeping, or engaging in any activity that sustains the body or promotes the common good, do they consider their actions to be good works pleasing to God? You will find that they say no. They define good works very narrowly and confine them to church-related activities such as praying, fasting, and giving alms.[1]

The idea for this book was born in a church basement. I was talking to a group of adults at a congregational forum. I was speaking on Reformation Sunday and my charge was, on the surface, simple enough: explain why Martin Luther is important to the church of today. I started my talk with Luther's own life story and his spiritual crisis within the monastery. Next, we traced his rediscovery of Paul's message of justification by faith alone. And then, I made a wrong move—I began to go into some detail about the various theories of justification in the late medieval church and how Luther's views differed from them. As a church historian, this topic was interesting to me. I love tracing the nuances of historical theology and I make no apology for that. It is

---

1. Martin Luther, *Treatise on Good Works* (1520) trans. and introduced by Scott H. Hendrix (Minneapolis: Fortress Press, 2012), 20.

1

important for students of theology to understand the major doctrines of the church.

But most of those in my church basement audience clearly understood Luther's message. They may not have known the subtleties of Thomas Aquinas or William of Ockham, but they did grasp the essential truth: that God, as revealed in Jesus Christ, loves the unlovable. However, they probably did not need to hear that morning about the distinction between congruent and condign merit. I saw it in their faces. Moreover, I knew some of folks personally. They were most likely thinking the following: it is true that justification by faith is a great teaching—an amazing combination of comfort and freedom. But what happens when I go home? What does this mean for my relationship with my kids and my spouse? Does it have any bearing on my friendships? Can I take it to work with me? How does it affect my role in my community?

Please know that this is not yet another screed about the failure of academic theology to address the real issues of Christian life. Leaders in the church ought to be deeply grounded in the Bible and the Christian tradition. If anything, the need for a learned and intellectually nimble church leadership is more crucial than ever before. A postmodern world necessitates that Christians today are able to engage in a wide variety of conversations on the relationship between faith and science, faith and culture, faith and other religions, and so on.

But we also need to recognize that Luther regularly preached his theology. Justification was one side of the coin. And the other side was vocation.[2] Luther made sure that the Word became flesh in the actual lives of his people. He wanted them to understand that the great truth of God's love is carried

2. Marc Kolden, "Luther on Vocation," *Word and World* 3, No. 4 (Fall, 1983), 382–90.

to the farmer's field, the mason's quarry, and the midwife's birth chamber. And it is not only within the realm of work. Our callings extend to conversations with friends and the trials and joys of marriage and family life. Moreover, as I will argue, we have a special vocation to steward our own gifts by caring responsibly for ourselves.

Note that the title of the book is *Martin Luther and the Called Life*. The indebtedness to Luther in each chapter will be obvious. We will mine the reformer's life and theology for each topic covered. However, we also want to be careful about getting stuck in the sixteenth century. As we shall see, Luther had some wise things to say about marriage, work, citizenship, and so on. But he also said these things five hundred years ago. It was a time before the Enlightenment and the Industrial Revolution. Thus, it seems silly to expect that all of Luther's ideas translate well today. On some things (the role of women, for example), he was just wrong, or better still, a child of his own time. So, while each chapter will have a foundation in Luther's thinking, we will also use the reformer's own catechism question, "What Does This Mean?" in the second part of the book to ensure there is a vigorous engagement with life in the twenty-first century. These sections will not be an exhaustive review of the categories being explored, but rather, offer some pointers about how to think about our various callings in the present age. Luther is the catalyst for these observations, but they are not a commentary as such on the reformer's own views.

Some may resist using Luther as a guide for thinking about life today. After all, we are concerned with questions about meaning and purpose. Luther, however, wasn't concerned about "the meaning of life." This, of course, is true. A question about life's "meaning" is a modern concern. If anything,

Luther's life had too much meaning! His life was a desperate struggle for faith, where he was caught between the warring powers of God and Satan. But perhaps, the struggle with meaning and purpose in the twenty-first century is the result of limiting our horizons to the secular realm. Luther's teaching on vocation invites the reader to consider a theological perspective in addition to the ones normally used in sociology, politics, psychology, and so on. In fact, he believes that we can't help but be "religious" because everyone has to trust something to give meaning and value to life. Luther would identify that object as a "god."[3] Like it or not, Luther believed a theological perspective was hardwired into the human condition. When conceived this way, perhaps the distance between Luther's world and our own is not as far as first thought.

There are five reasons why a book such as this is needed. The first comes out of my experience of teaching religion to college undergraduates for the past twenty years. I am convinced, more than ever, that Luther is a bracing and exuberant alternative for what most of them conceive as "religion." The reigning paradigm for thinking about faith is what Christian Smith called moralistic therapeutic deism.[4] In other words, religion mainly has to do with being good (as you personally conceive it), maybe turning to God for comfort in a crisis, and otherwise seeing very little connection between this "faith" and daily life. Unfortunately, for most of my students, most of the time, God is absent. They struggle with questions of purpose and meaning, but often, fail to connect with religion—at least, one that is not idiosyncratic.

---

3. Martin Luther, "The Large Catechism" in BC:386–90.
4. Christian Smith with Melinda L. Denton, *Soul Searching: The Religious and Spiritual Lives of American Teenagers* (New York: Oxford University Press, 2005).

Luther's understanding of vocation is in complete opposition to this way of seeing life. To be sure, not everyone in my classroom embraces his views. But he provides a way of thinking about God and life that is not based on "performance," and in his teaching on vocation, he makes a case for a God who is present, a God who is deeply intertwined with creation.

Second, much attention has been paid to Luther's doctrine of justification. Luther himself invited this scrutiny when he declared in the Smalcald Articles that "nothing in this article can be conceded or given up."[5] For Luther, justification was the "chief article" and he drew the sharpest possible line between the righteousness given to us by God in Christ and the human righteousness that is exercised for the sake of the world.[6] In other words, God declares the sinner righteous—it is a powerful Word that transforms the sinner, and yet, it is a Word that remains outside of the recipient. One becomes holy because of one's relationship to Christ and not because a person has changed to become more like Christ. This is in contrast to alternatives to justification that emphasize the transformation of the sinner into a state of greater "holiness."[7]

This is the doctrine I was taught, and, when preached rightly, is powerful. However, being declared righteous in Christ does not happen in the abstract. It occurs to men and women living real lives in the midst of families, friendships, work, and communities. Without an understanding of vocation, the earthly corollary to justification, the Word may enter the mind, but it really doesn't return the justified sinner to the created world of real life. The earthly callings of

5. Martin Luther, "The Smalcald Articles," in BC:301.
6. Ibid.
7. See Gerhard Forde's *Justification by Faith: A Matter of Death and Life* (Philadelphia: Fortress Press, 1982) for a clear and masterful treatment of this important issue.

Christians need more attention than they have typically received. As we shall see, we have no better role model than the preaching of Martin Luther himself. The reformer's sermons are crowded with references to the vocation of his listeners.[8]

Third, there have been no book-length treatments of Luther's doctrine of vocation in English since Gustaf Wingren's magisterial *Luther on Vocation*.[9] This text has stood the test of time and remains an invaluable reference for anyone interested in a serious engagement with Luther's teaching. But it was first published in 1943 (it was Wingren's doctoral dissertation—English translation in 1957) and much has changed since the world was embroiled in the Second World War. Also, Wingren's text is especially strong for its investigation of the vertical relationship between God and the believer. The focus is on how faith leads to earthly service and how the latter, in turn, affects the former. Wingren's insights on these issues are profound and still deserve close consideration. But there is less attention paid to the actual callings of Christians in the world.

Most of what has been written by others seems to conflate earthly vocation with work. The writings of Gene Veith are an exception.[10] But even Veith has a modest amount to say about Luther's own views, and rather, keeps the spotlight on

---

8. Robert Kolb, *Luther and the Stories of God. Biblical Narratives as a Foundation for Christian Living* (Grand Rapids: Baker Academic, 2012). See especially chapter six.

9. Gustaf Wingren, *Luther on Vocation*, trans. by Carl C. Rasmussen (Philadelphia: Muhlenburg Press, 1957).

10. Among his many books see *God at Work: Your Christian Vocation in All of Life* (Wheaton: Crossways, 2002) and *The Spirituality of the Cross: The Way of the First Evangelicals* (St. Louis: Concordia, 1999). Mention must also be made of the work of Robert Benne and his *Ordinary Saints: An Introduction to the Christian Life* (Minneapolis: Fortress Press, 2003). This is a great resource on vocation and Benne's indebtedness to the Lutheran tradition is clear. He also links a sense of calling with life beyond work. But Benne's purpose is not to explore Luther's own vocation. Another good book is Douglas Schuurman's *Vocation: Discerning Our Callings in Life* (Grand Rapids: Eerdmans, 2004).

contemporary application. The present work will ground its views in Luther's own life story, and then, make connections with modern life.

Fourth, while many Christian churches have embraced an understanding of vocation and see it as central to their work, there has also been a tendency to concentrate on what might be called a "heroic" view of the concept. In this perspective, it is demanded that we link vocation almost exclusively with a challenge to injustice in the world. The calling of Christians is to speak up for the voiceless, include those pressed to the margins, and to work to end poverty and the desecration of the environment.

There needs to be great care taken when discussing this topic. The church must address issues such as poverty, the environment, and discrimination. Our society needs faith communities to be a moral beacon and point out truths that discomfort, startle, and cause unease. After all, Jesus issues the call. According to the gospel of Luke (4:18–19), here are the first words of his public ministry:

> The Spirit of the Lord is upon me, because he has anointed me to bring good news to the poor. He has sent me to proclaim release to the captives and recovery of sight to the blind, to let the oppressed go free, to proclaim the year of the Lord's favor.

However, there also needs to be recognition that our public witness concerning injustice is only one part of our actual vocation. Ninety percent or more of our time is spent in the nitty-gritty of life, far out of the spotlight. Marriage and family life demand large amounts of time that involve the arts of discretion, negotiation, compromise, and forgiveness. Friendships need to be nurtured, often by means of a listening ear. In our work, less than dramatic details need significant attention. As I tell my students, their most important calling is to be the best learners they can possibly be: turn off the phones, do the readings, avoid sloth, show up in class, and participate in discussions. There is nothing very glamorous about any of that, but it is still a difficult calling to live up to.

It is my hope that this book can provide a corrective to this heroic concept of vocation. That will be a delicate task. After all, the Lutheran tradition has often been accused of quietism in its public witness.[11] The last thing needed is a return to a "private" faith that makes no connection with public life. But we also need to make room for a sense of calling in the large spaces of life that have been vacated by some churches and theological scholarship.

Fifth, and finally, I believe this book is timely. In 2017 the Lutheran church celebrates the 500th anniversary of Luther's posting of the Ninety-Five Theses. Conversation and questions about Luther will only increase in churches and in the larger public realm. This is a great opportunity for those familiar with Luther and his theology to take yet another look at him through the less well-known lens of vocation. And for those not acquainted with Luther, there is no better place to begin study of him than with his reflections on how the Christian faith is lived out in daily life.

Furthermore, vocation has become a hot topic in many colleges and universities of the church. The reason for much of this increased attention is a multi-million-dollar effort by the Lilly Endowment to provide grants to schools in order to integrate vocation into the lives of their institutions.[12] As a

---

11. See William Lazareth's *Christians in Society. Luther, the Bible and Social Ethics* (Minneapolis: Fortress Press, 2001), 2–30.

12. Since 2000, the Lilly Endowment has awarded nearly one hundred grants to church-related colleges and universities interested in making a theological understanding of vocation integral to their mission. My school, Augsburg College of Minneapolis, was the recipient of one of these grants.

result, there has been a significant increase in discussion about the meaning of vocation—a good thing.

But sometimes this conversation lacks the proper rooting in the Christian tradition. Indeed, it has been my experience that the concept is vulnerable to a phenomenon that might be called "vocation lite." This happens when the notion of a calling is cut loose from its theological moorings and is interpreted exclusively in therapeutic or psychological categories. To be clear, it is possible to talk about vocation in a meaningful way beyond the boundaries of the Lutheran and Christian heritage. But that tradition has some important things to say about vocation that need to be kept in mind by anyone seeking to interpret it for an audience in the twenty-first century.

So, this is a book on Luther's theology of vocation in the context of his own life. It begins by setting Luther's thinking within the late medieval world (1300–1500)—a time that cannot be understood itself without a glance back at the Greek roots of Western civilization. We will examine how Luther's own sense of calling as a teacher and preacher developed out of his time in the monastery. Then, we will describe his theology of vocation, seeking to ground his views within the comfort and challenge of baptism. As Luther overturned the sacramental system of the late medieval church, he needed a new foundation for how to relate our salvation in Christ to our life in Christ. He found it in baptism, where the Christian daily dies and rises with Christ.

The second part of the book will look at the various arenas to which a Christian is called. In each chapter, we will begin with Luther's own story, and then, ask, "What does this mean?" for Christians today. Perhaps surprising to some, we will begin with the individual. This is not a concession to modern individualism, but, as we shall see, the very place where Luther himself begins to discuss the meaning of Christian life in the world. We then proceed to look at the various dimensions of the Christian's calling beyond the self. We will honor Luther's categories (he saw three basic "orders" in life—the domestic, civil, and ecclesiastical), but stretch them in a way that provides engagement with contemporary life. Basically, we will move in outwardly expanding concentric circles. Christ crucified, to whom we are joined in baptism, remains at the center.

Following the individual's vocation, we move to what Luther called the "domestic realm." There has been significant attention devoted to Luther's marriage to Katherine von Bora. Until fairly recently, there has been a tendency to sentimentalize "Katie" Luther as the ideal "housewife." Many accounts ignored the harsh realities of women's experience in the sixteenth century. Recent scholarship allows us a more realistic view of Luther's marriage.[13] Some of what he says about the calling of a husband or wife simply reflects his sixteenth-century context and is no longer applicable. But there is much in Luther's marriage that can still be instructive for today.

It is sometimes forgotten that Luther was not only married, but was also a father and a son. A generation ago, Erik Erikson's *Young Man Luther* generated much controversy about the reformer's relationship with the father.[14] We will not revisit that dispute in any type of involved way, but rather, look at

---

13. See Susan C. Karant-Nunn and Merry E. Wiesner-Hanks, *Luther on Women: A Sourcebook* (Cambridge, UK: Cambridge University Press, 2003).
14. Erik H. Erikson, *Young Man Luther; A Study in Psychoanalysis and History* (New York: Norton, 1958). Erikson's thesis was that Luther's rebellion against the teaching of the church was rooted in his complicated relationship with his father.

Luther's actions as a son and a father and see how they might speak to those callings today.

Next, we move beyond the realm of home in order to look at the civil realm. The meaning of our calling to be citizens will be discussed here. Luther lived long before the advent of Jeffersonian democracy. So, we should not expect him to reflect the values of the United Nations charter on human rights. However, his two kingdoms theory (much misunderstood) can still serve as a helpful model for how to think about the relationship of faith and politics. Contrary to popular notions, Luther believed deeply that faith ought to be exercised in the political realm. His insights in this area can help us discern the calling of the Christian as one seeks to love the neighbor in the civil community.

Also to be examined is the calling of the Christian in the congregation. Luther is best known as the bold reformer who challenged the corruption and greed of the late medieval church. However, Luther not only operated on a grand historical stage, but was deeply involved in the parish life of the church in his home city of Wittenberg. From his preaching, we gain a good idea of what it means to participate in a Christian community. We also need to ask ourselves: What does it mean to be called to be a faithful member of a congregation? How does the congregation sometimes frustrate an understanding of vocation? How important is a congregational connection and worship itself for nurturing a sense of calling?

While it was technically part of Luther's understanding of the domestic realm, we will link work more directly with the outside world because that is a better reflection of modern sensibilities. In many contemporary accounts of vocation, this becomes equated with "calling." In other words, vocation equals a job. As we have suggested, this was not the case with Luther. His revolution against the late medieval church's view of vocation certainly had huge implications for work, and we will describe how Luther's theology ennobled the entire realm of labor. For Luther himself, it will mean looking at his own efforts as a scholar and teacher. But this discussion will be set against a horizon that views vocation as something that includes all of life's activity and not just work alone.

There is little doubt that each of these proposed chapters on the various realms of vocation could be a book in itself. Moreover, the secondary literature on Luther's life and theology is nothing short of overwhelming. Indeed, as some writers have said, Luther is an "ocean." His own voluminous writings (120 volumes in the Weimar edition) have been exceeded exponentially by his interpreters. So, none of these chapters aspires to be the final word on Luther's ideas about vocation. Furthermore, the goal is to make this work accessible to the nonscholar. There is something ironic about a book on Luther's views on vocation that is intended only for the specialist. The whole point is to help people see how Luther might help them in thinking about their own callings as spouses, parents, citizens, church members, and workers.

PART I

Luther's Calling

1

The Second Baptism is First

Therefore, the Christian life is not about what the monks claim—that it means sending people into the wilderness or cloister. On the contrary, the Christian life leads you to those who need your works.[1]

The spiritual orders, particularly those who live in monasteries and nunneries, brag that they lead contemplative lives. Well, they know as much about a contemplative life as a goose knows of the Psalter . . . our Lord has not commanded that we sit around and gaze up at heaven. Instead of a focus on a contemplative life God has commanded us to lead an active life in the world in faith, love and bearing of the cross.[2]

Life in the Western world in the late Middle Ages (1300–1500) can be likened to a three-story home. God and the heavenly court reside on the top floor. Beneath the Lord, on the middle level, are the religious people—monks, priests, nuns—who, by

---

1. Martin Luther, "Sermon on the Fourth Sunday after Trinity" (1529), *WA* 29:403. Translation mine.
2. Martin Luther, "Sermon on Day of St. John" (1527), *WA* 17(2):349. Translation mine.

virtue of their vows, have callings or vocations. Their public declarations to lead holy lives, characterized by poverty, chastity, and obedience, put them closer to their Creator and also provide greater assurance of blessed entrance into God's kingdom at the end of their lives. On the ground floor is the vast multitude of humanity. They are the folks who keep life going—the merchants, farmers, blacksmiths, midwives, mothers, and fathers. They are said to lack vocations because their daily activities inevitably involve worldly compromise that dilutes the pure love of God.

How did things come to be this way? In this opening chapter, we will describe how the church understood vocation on the eve of the Reformation. This will require a sweeping overview of some key developments in the previous two thousand years. We will begin by looking at thought world of the Greeks. This section will be followed by a review of biblical material on vocation, noting its centrality to the message of the Scriptures. And then, in a peculiar twist, we will see how the classical and biblical views were combined in a way that limited a sense of calling to a particular class of people. Also examined will be the church's sacramental system, especially baptism and penance, for both provide significant insights into the thought worlds of medieval men and women.

The Greeks

As many writers have noted, there has been a deep chasm in the Western tradition between the "thinkers" and the "doers," or the contemplative and the active life. In a way, this makes sense intuitively. Human beings are different from the rest of the animal kingdom. We have the ability to reason and this sets us apart from other creatures. Given this capability, it is not surprising that rational thought would be elevated above physical life. And this is exactly what happened in Greek philosophy, which was highly influential in the Western intellectual tradition.

For Plato, the external world, which we know by our senses, is subject to change and decay. The saying "the only thing that is permanent is change" reflects this viewpoint. Humans and animals are born, grow and develop, and eventually, die. The natural world around us reflects a similar pattern. Even the hardest of stones eventually grinds into dust. But this did not mean everything was changing and temporary. Plato believed we had access to another realm (he called it the "forms") when we turn away from our senses (which only provide knowledge of the changing world) and focus instead on our souls, which provide contact with the eternal.

This act of turning inward or the undertaking of reflection was the first step of what the Greeks called "philosophy," or the search for wisdom. They believed that the thought required to contemplate truth also implied leisure. The act of "doing" philosophy was not a "hobby" for the Greeks. It required strenuous effort and discipline. Naturally, it also meant that one had to be set apart from the distractions of the world. Making a living or looking after a household left no time to pursue this ideal. Moreover, the body also hinders the mind in its quest for wisdom. It is incessantly making demands—it needs food, clothing, exercise, and rest. Paying attention to the body can deflect from the contemplative life.

Now, it is obvious that the vast majority of human beings will not have the luxury of leading a life dedicated to philosophy. Plato and his followers recognized this. Many humans were consigned to a life of manual labor and most of the people in this group were slaves. A smaller number led a higher type of life. They were the political leaders who organized society and provided security for the community. But then, there are the rare few who lead genuine philosophical lives. They benefit from the labor of the slave and the managerial skills of the politicians. But it is their contemplation of things divine and eternal that sets them apart.

The Biblical Context

Jews and Christians have long recognized that a central characteristic of God in the Bible is that of one who speaks or calls. For example, the opening chapter of Genesis reveals a God who creates by speaking. There are fourteen references to God speaking or calling in the first twenty-nine verses. Furthermore, Genesis 1 suggests that when God speaks, the effect is powerful and transformative. After all, it is possible to talk and have nothing happen. This is not the case with God's speech. At the beginning of each day of creation stands the phrase "And God said . . . ," which is followed by yet more details being added to earth's majestic landscape. The crowning achievement of God is the creation of humanity (Genesis 1:26), which, like rest of the world, is a result of divine speech and is made in God's very image.[3]

The completion of creation does not result in divine silence. It is the conviction of the Scriptures that the God who speaks continues to be active in the world. Genesis also tells us that God calls the nation of Israel into existence and assigns her the task of being his witness in the world. Moreover, it is important to notice that God's call to Israel is not abstract or general; it is

---

3. Walter Brueggemann, *Genesis. A Bible Commentary for Preaching and Teaching* (Atlanta: John Knox Press, 1982), 1–39. Brueggemann organizes his entire commentary on Genesis around the theme of God's call.

individuals who hear God's voice and respond in various ways. It might be instructive to cite several examples.

The call of Abraham and Sarah is immediate and direct. God says, "Go from your country and your kindred and your father's house to the land that I will show you and I will make of you a great nation and bless you." And the text simply reports that Abraham "went as the Lord had told him" (Genesis 12:1-4). But other calls tend to be more complicated.

God calls Moses dramatically through a burning bush. Upon hearing the identity of the voice, Moses hides his face, fearing the presence of the Holy One of Israel. However, following this initial encounter, the relationship between God and Moses becomes much more mundane and conflicted. God commissions Moses to deliver his people out of the hands of the Pharaoh. But Moses exhibits great reluctance to answer the call. He raises five separate objections to the task God has presented him. Finally, God becomes exasperated with Moses's excuses and the reluctant leader of Israel is forced to yield to the divine will.[4]

The prophet Jonah illustrates yet another way of responding to God's call. When he is told by God to go to Nineveh and speak a word of judgment, Jonah flees in the opposite direction. When God foils his travel plans (and the prophet becomes well acquainted with a large fish), Jonah ends up acquiescing to God's command and preaches to the wicked city of Nineveh. To his total surprise, his preaching is effective. Nineveh repents and avoids divine retribution. Interestingly, Jonah is completely undone by this turn of events and becomes angry at God for showing mercy and forbearance.

Two examples from the New Testament are also instructive

---

4. See Terence E. Fretheim, *Exodus. A Bible Commentary for Teaching and Preaching* (Louisville: John Knox Press, 1991), 51–82.

for reflecting on the call of God. Mary is greatly troubled and afraid when she hears the greeting of the angel Gabriel. After learning that she is to be the mother of Jesus, her next reaction is to question the possibility of such a birth, given her virginity. Only after repeated assurances from the angelic messenger does she submit to the divine plan. The call of Jesus' disciples echoes the divine power displayed in the speech of creation. When Jesus sees Simon and Andrew casting nets into the sea, he summons them to follow. The reader is given no hint of hesitation; the fishermen hear the voice of Jesus and they immediately follow. A similar pattern of call and immediate response is repeated with the disciples James and John. These narratives impress upon the reader the irresistible force of Jesus' words and the way his speech results in a decisive break with the past As Dietrich Bonhoeffer notes of this text: "This encounter (with the disciples) is a testimony to the absolute, direct, and unaccountable authority of Jesus. There is no need of any preliminaries, and no other consequence but obedience to the call."[5]

These biblical reflections on the call are but a small sampling of the available material. Much more could be said about the centrality of vocation within the authoritative texts of the Judeo-Christian tradition. But based on the material provided, we might draw the following conclusions about the shape and content of vocation in the Bible.

The God of the Bible is one who speaks. Fundamental to the character of God is speaking. The Scriptures witness time and again to a God who makes himself known through speech. This has significant consequences for the way a reader approaches the Bible. Instead of assuming a role of mastery over the text, where the primary goal is to probe and discover

5. Dietrich Bonhoeffer, *The Cost of Discipleship* (New York: MacMillian, 1959), 57.

what a particular passage means, the student of the Bible, informed by a sense of vocation, begins with an attitude of expectant listening. The way to God may first be through our ears rather than a critical busyness that misses what God is actually trying to say. A sense of vocation or calling can only be nurtured if one is first attentive to the divine voice that speaks through the words of the Bible.

God's speech is powerful. As we have seen, Genesis 1 presents a God who speaks with powerful effect. These are not empty words to fill time while waiting for some meaningful activity to take place. The words themselves are the activity. They create and transform reality. As many have pointed out, the language of the Bible is not only informative or descriptive. In many cases, it is also "performative." In other words, the speech of Scripture has the power to effect change in the most profound way (Isaiah 55:10–11). Thus, one who listens for the voice of God in Scripture must be prepared for the power of the words addressed to the listener. In the realm of vocation, one enters a world that upends traditional ways of seeing reality and reorganizes priorities. Vocation has little in common with the typical human pursuits of comfort, security, and stability.

God's call can be resisted. While several of the biblical figures addressed by God appear to respond to the call with unquestioning obedience, some of the examples noted above indicate a less than enthusiastic reaction to the divine summons. Moses is perhaps the most famous example of reluctance in vocation. Before eventually trying God's patience, he invokes numerous excuses to avoid the assignment given to him. Jonah tries to ignore the call altogether before he discovers the futility of fleeing from the God of all creation. These examples are useful. While the Bible accentuates the power of God's speech, it is not the case that humans are simply automatons without wills of their own. Thus, evidence of resistance in a calling should not be a cause for undue alarm. The Bible provides numerous cases of people whom God used in spite of their reluctance to answer the call.

God's call can be ambiguous. Mary's fear upon hearing the words of the angel Gabriel can serve as a lens for those whom a sense of calling is uncertain or tenuous. There is plenty of room in the concept of vocation for hesitation, questioning, and puzzlement. Even those who take up a stance of "expectant listening" find themselves in significant periods of divine silence. Or they may feel there are too many voices in their lives, and thus, find it difficult to sort out what constitutes a genuine call. To be avoided, however, is the modern tendency to wallow in ambiguity. While acknowledging the difficulty of discernment, the concept of vocation insists that God has spoken and continues to speak. Our hardness of hearing should not yield to a belief that God has stopped speaking.

God's call comes in the context of community. While the call comes to individuals in the Bible, it is never received in isolation. Vocation is always connected with a mission for the larger community. God summons Moses so that he might lead the people of Israel out of bondage. Mary is called so that she might bear the one who fulfills God's promises to Israel and the world. The disciples are called so that they might constitute the beginnings of a new community charged with telling the world of a new way that God has acted in the person of Jesus of Nazareth. Underscored here is the dramatic difference between vocation and some modern strains of individualism. In vocation, the individual never stands alone. Rather, the one called is continually acting in the world and responding to the claims of God and the larger community.

God's call is gracious. This needs to be the last word in our summary comments about vocation in the Scriptures. Those in the realm of vocation often find themselves in bewildering circumstances. God tells Abraham: "Leave *your* country and *your* kindred and *your* father's house (emphasis mine) . . ." (Genesis 12:1). Embracing the call can mean a heartrending suffering where the familiar gives way to loneliness and alienation. Therefore, it is crucial to remind ourselves that the God who calls us is also a God who fundamentally favors us. The promises of Scripture point to a God who not only calls us, but a God who keeps and preserves us. For the Christian faith, this is highlighted most dramatically in the death and resurrection of Jesus of Nazareth. Here, we have a model of one who takes all human opposition to God upon himself and is thereby driven to death. In a remarkable reversal, however, death does not have the final word. At the heart of the Christian confession is the belief that God has raised Jesus from the dead, and thus, vindicated his mission. Upon hearing the gracious voice of Christ in vocation, Christians are empowered to move beyond themselves and live lives of service and love.

The Early Christian World

It is hard to overestimate the influence that the Greeks had on the early Christian church. It could be said that Greek philosophy (like that sketched above) was intertwined with the world of antiquity in a way similar to how an idea like evolution is part of our own. In other words, it would be extremely difficult for early Christian writers to think about themselves and their world in a way that substantially escaped this framework.

Two opposing forces seem to be at work. On the one hand,

there is the goodness of creation and the confession that the Word has become flesh. God's deep commitment to creation, culminating in the incarnation (God becoming *flesh*) in Jesus of Nazareth, certainly puts a strain on the Greek tendency to separate the material and spiritual realms. But the incarnation of Christ was also accompanied by biblical texts that encouraged the followers of Jesus to "sell all you own and distribute the money to the poor, and you will have treasure in heaven; then come, follow me" (Luke 18:22). Here, there is a call for a rigorous denial of the self and an admonition to focus one's attention beyond the material world. The early Christians saw the earthly order as good, but also fraught with danger and temptation.

The tension of being "in the world but not of it" was not a big problem for the first followers of Jesus. Many knew first-hand the cost of following Christ. A frequently hostile Roman Empire meant persecution for one's beliefs and even martyrdom was a real possibility. But what happens when Christianity eventually becomes legal in the empire (as was the case after the conversion of the Emperor Constantine in 313)? The call for self-denial becomes more difficult to achieve when being a Christian might now confer societal advantages. Thus, it is not surprising that the elevation of Christianity's status in the culture will correspond to a rising interest in monasticism. The Greek ideal of retreat from the world of activity to a life of contemplation merges with the stern demands of the gospel for Christians to "to deny themselves and take up their cross."

As a result, a separate class of elite Christians begins to emerge. While there is certainly recognition of oneness in Christ, within that unity, there emerges two distinct ways of being Christian. The fourth-century church father, Eusebius, expresses it well:

Two ways of life were thus given by the Lord to His Church. The one is above nature, and beyond common living; it admits not marriage, child-bearing, property nor the possession of wealth. . . . Like some celestial beings, these gaze down upon human life, performing a duty of priesthood to almighty God for the whole race. . . . And the more humble, more human way prompts men to join in pure nuptials, and to produce children, to undertake government, to give orders to soldiers fighting for right; it allows them to have minds for farming, for trade and for the other more secular interests as well as for religion.[6]

The Middle Ages

There is no better example of the way "above nature" than that of monasticism. In the West, it was given form and shape by Benedict of Nursia (480–543). His Rule or list of obligations for monks became the standard for cloistered communities. Commitment to the monastic life involved a vow of poverty, chastity, and obedience. In many communities, this meant a renunciation of all private property, a determination to live "purely" (with a special emphasis on celibacy), and unwavering allegiance to the abbot or the head of the order. It should also be noted that an order for women was established shortly after Benedict's death.

---

6. As quoted in Peter R. L. Brown, *The Body and Society Men, Women, and Sexual Renunciation in Early Christianity* (New York: Columbia University Press, 1988), 205.

Benedict of Nursia. Courtesy of Wikimedia Commons.

There is no question that monasteries were complex communities. They were not only places "set apart" for prayer and contemplation. The monks and nuns worried about the temptations associated with idleness. They also needed to tend to the daily needs of life. Accordingly, monasteries often encompassed vineyards, breweries, and farms. Monks and nuns milked cows and grew crops. Often, they established schools for the surrounding area. Monasteries and cloisters were places of refuge for those fleeing persecution. They often served as hospitals for the ill.

Furthermore, as the Middle Ages progressed, the monastic way of life became increasingly popular. This will not surprise visitors to Europe today. Scattered among the cities and countryside are the remnants of this once thriving institution. Moreover, the so-called mendicant orders, such as the Franciscans and Dominicans, moved beyond the monastery walls and into communities as preachers and teachers. This meant the monastic way of life had a greater influence on laity.

All this should not obscure the prime purpose of the life of a monk or nun: union of the soul with God. An active life of work can be found within the monastery's walls, but the rationale for such activity is the support of the contemplative life. Separation from the world is largely for the sake of salvation. Bernard of Clairvaux's work, *On Loving God*, is an excellent expression of this ideal. As the historian Steven Ozment summarizes Bernard's work, the discipline of the monastery is designed to move a person in four stages from: 1) a love of self to, 2) love of God based on fear to, 3) love of God based partly on fear and partly on trust to, 4) pure love of God founded solely on the fact that God ought to loved for God's sake and not anything that might be gained by humans.[7]

There is little doubt in the minds of the major theologians of the period about the superiority of monastic life. The greatest thinker of the Middle Ages, Thomas Aquinas (1225–74), believed those who dedicated themselves to poverty, chastity, and obedience had chosen the more perfect way. Monks were freed from the distractions of domestic responsibilities and the

---

7. Steven Ozment, *The Age of Reform, 1250–1550* (New Haven and London: Yale University Press, 1980), 87–89.

temptations of the world. This enabled them to love God more purely.[8] Aquinas even regarded the monastic vow as equivalent to a second baptism, meaning that it forgave all sins committed up to that point in life.[9] And, according to the aforementioned Bernard, the diligent obedience of a monk restored the divine image lost in the Garden of Eden and even elevated him near the realm of the angels.[10] Overall, it might be said that monks and nuns are the ultimate spiritual athletes. Equipped with the tools of fasting, prayer, daily worship, and confession, they directed their souls heavenward in a process both arduous and disciplined as well as one that reflected a more perfect way of life.

Those in cloisters not only lived a superior way of life, but their spiritual ideals came to dominate the imaginations of all people when it came to the question of how to live as a Christian. By the thirteenth century, the ordinary Christian saw one's life through a sacramental lens. At this time, the church had settled on seven sacraments—baptism, penance (confession), Eucharist, confirmation, marriage, ordination, and extreme unction (or "last rites"). But the most important were baptism, penance, and Eucharist.

All Christians at this time had their children baptized shortly after birth. Baptism's purpose was to wash away original sin (which infected the whole human race or all the children of Adam and Eve). It was taken with utmost seriousness because infant mortality rates were high. You could not take a chance on having a child die before receiving baptism. However, for sins committed after baptism, the medieval Christian looked to the sacrament of penance. The church mandated confession to

8. St. Thomas Aquinas, *Summa Theologica*, II, 2nd, Q. 186, art. 7 in *Introduction to St. Thomas Aquinas*, ed. by Anton C. Pegis (New York: Modern Library, 1948).
9. Ibid., II, 2nd, Q. 189, art. 3.
10. Ozment, *Age of Reform*, 85.

a priest annually in the early thirteenth century. Furthermore, participation in the most holy Eucharist, where one communed with the very body and blood of Christ, dictated a need in many consciences to purify oneself as much as humanly possible.

There is significant evidence suggesting the church often failed the people at this crucial sacramental juncture.[11] The goal was to communicate God's grace and forgiveness. The importance of penance needs to be underlined. Baptism, though necessary, was confined to infancy. Confession, thus, became a significant intersection between the church and the people. Ideally, the rhythm of the Christian life in the medieval church was governed by confession and the eucharist. At least once a year, but probably more frequently, a person confessed to a priest and received the body and blood of Christ.

But, as noted, the process of penance often frustrated those receiving the sacrament. The first part of penance entails remorse or contrition for one's sin and confession to a priest. Clerics would often use confessional manuals consisting of questions designed to scour the consciences of the penitent. The questions themselves often reflected the concerns of monastic/clerical piety since the authors of the guides were priests or monks themselves. This probably meant a significant disconnect between the experience of lay people and the concerns of the church. The initial step of confession was followed by priestly absolution of sins. But the process was still not complete. The sacrament still needed to be "completed" by a work of satisfaction. In other words, the penitent was expected to do "penance" or repay the debt incurred by one's sin. The act of penance corresponded to the gravity of the sin. The worse the offense, the more burdensome the penance. Of

11. Robert Kolb and Charles P. Arand, *The Genius of Luther's Theology* (Grand Rapids: Baker Academic, 2008), 33–35.

29

course, the whole system needed a ranking of sins to work. Elaborate lists were developed to help priests and penitents determine the right penance.[12]

Additionally, the overarching theological structure often made things worse. The two main options (shaped by Thomas Aquinas and William of Ockham, respectively) put a significant burden on the Christian to at least do *something* of their own free will to cooperate in the process of salvation. For sensitive consciences, this opened the door to the question: How much must I do? And how can I know when I have done enough? These are the very questions that would trouble Luther in the monastery. As we shall see, he became convinced that the uncertainty created by these theologies meant that the goodness of God was called into question. In response, he inaugurated a theological revolution that entailed a whole new way of thinking about God and the place of human activity in the world.

Let's review some of the main points in this chapter. We began by looking at the Greeks and their conviction that the contemplative life was superior to the practical world of work and labor. Then, we saw the centrality of a sense of calling in the Bible, rooted in a gracious God who speaks to humanity, even though the latter is sometimes hard of hearing. As Christianity gained power as an institution in the West, there was a corresponding desire to maintain a "pure" version of the faith, untainted by worldly concerns. In many ways, monasticism becomes the religious equivalent of the Greek ideal. Monks and nuns are often "cloistered" (from the Latin,

---

12. For an excellent overview of the penitential process, see *Handbook for Curates. A Late Medieval Manual on Pastoral Ministry*, trans. by Anne T. Thayer (Washington, DC: The Catholic University Press, 2011), 157–269. Another good resource is Thomas Tentler's *Sin and Confession on the Eve of the Reformation* (Princeton: Princeton University Press, 1977).

meaning "to enclose") so that they can live a spiritually elite life, unavailable to those in the secular world. They alone are said to have vocations or callings because of the supposed purity of their love of God. Moreover, their spiritual goals season the understanding of the church's sacramental life, particularly the all-important rites of penance and the eucharist.

It might be helpful to conclude with a concrete image from the Bible: the story of Jesus' visit to Mary and Martha. As many readers will recall, Jesus comes to the home of the sisters, Mary and Martha. Mary sits at Jesus' feet and listens to him while Martha is busy making the house ready for their esteemed guest. When Martha complains about Mary's lack of assistance, Jesus gently corrects her: "Martha, Martha, you are worried and distracted by many things; there is need of only one thing. Mary has chosen the better part, which will not be taken away from her" (Luke 10:38–42).

For Thomas Aquinas, this story is a clear indication that Jesus preferred the contemplative life to the active one. In effect, Jesus' praise of Mary is another way of elevating the vocation of the monk or nun over those left behind in the world.[13] Mary has a calling. She becomes the image of the true disciple of Christ while Martha, preoccupied with the tasks of daily life, is unable to devote herself fully to God. As we come to Martin Luther and the Reformation, we will see that his new understanding of vocation leads him to interpret this text in a different way. For Luther, Mary is the picture of the faithful Christian who listens carefully to God's Word. Martha mistakenly busies herself with works and fails to attend to the preaching of Christ. Instead of using the story to illustrate the superiority of the contemplative life, Luther underscores

---

13. Aquinas, *Summa*, II, 2nd, Q. 182, art. 1 in *Introduction to St. Thomas*, ed. by Pegis.

the importance of faith and how it precedes good works. Most telling, neither Mary nor Martha is closer to God by virtue of the place or station they occupy in life.[14]

14. Karant-Nunn and Wiesner-Hanks, *Luther on Women*, 60, 78–80.

2

Luther: His Road to Vocation

His Road to Vocation

How is it possible that you are not called? You are always in some sort of position. You have always been a husband or a wife or a son or a daughter or a servant. Imagine the lowest position—as a husband do you not have enough to do to watch over your spouse, children, workers and property so that all might be obedient to God and no harm comes to any of them? Indeed, even if you had four heads and ten hands you would scarcely have the energy for such a task. And I guarantee you would not be thinking about making a pilgrimage or doing some so-called "saintly" work.[1]

Life without Vocation

It may seem odd to say it this way, but according to the standards of the late Middle Ages, Martin Luther initially lacked a vocation. To be sure, he was baptized on November

---

1. Martin Luther, "Sermon on John 21:19–24" (1522), in *WA* 10 (I):308. Translation mine.

11, 1483, which was the day after his birth. But for the next twenty two years, Luther lacked a calling. The same holds true for his parents.

Hans and Margaret Luther were hardworking folks who lived close to the land. We have paintings of them by the famous artist, Lucas Cranach. Both faces are creased with care and the burden of work. Their hands are thick and rough. Save for a fur collar on Hans, there are no signs of wealth or accomplishment. It is clear that life was not easy for either of Luther's parents.

His father initially labored in the copper mines in the region of Saxony in the northern part of Germany. It was hard and dangerous work. He evidently was industrious as he even came to own several of the mines by the time Luther became a young man. While never prosperous, he did make enough money to send Luther to school—a luxury the illiterate Hans never enjoyed.

His mother tended to the home, which in itself was a difficult task in the sixteenth century. The life of women such as Margaret was centered on raising a family and the difficult task of managing a household. Hard work defined the day. Having children was hazardous. Not only was an infant's life fragile (maybe half made it to the first birthday), but also, the act of giving birth exposed the woman to the primitive world of medieval medicine. Dying during childbirth was not an uncommon experience.

Luther benefitted from his parents' industry and thrift. They had enough money to send him to various schools, where he proved himself a fine student. Finally, in 1505, at the age of twenty-two, he received his master's degree from the University of Erfurt, where he had been studying the previous four years. He was now qualified to enter one of the three so-called "professional" schools of that time. He could study medicine, law, or theology. Not surprisingly, he picked law. This was probably in accordance with the wishes of his parents. For example, we know that his father Hans spent a huge sum on an expensive set of law books to give to his son. By becoming a lawyer, Luther would rise above the rough life of a miner. Moreover, he could support his parents in their old age. There was no such thing as social security in the sixteenth century! If successful in law, Luther might enjoy the income and prestige that came from working in a princely court or in the office of a local bishop. To put it bluntly, a law degree meant access to money and power.

We began this section by suggesting that neither Luther nor his parents had a vocation, as this was commonly understood in their age. This is not to trivialize Luther's early life. He had important roles as a son and a student. Hans and Margaret were a father and mother to him, respectively. Hans labored hard in the earth, extracting its treasures for use in the developing economy. It is difficult to imagine a job more dangerous than that of a sixteenth-century copper miner. Margaret managed the household—which, in all likelihood, meant keeping a significant garden, bargaining in the markets, preparing meals, watching budgets, caring for livestock, and raising children.

The church of the day understood these tasks were important. All were needed to sustain life on this earth. But that was also the point—they were activities centered on *this* life on *this* earth. People needed to raise children, work, feed, and educate themselves. But it was a secondary concern, next to the real purpose of earthly life—the preparation of one's soul for next life. As the church saw it, the people who took this seriously were the ones who had *vocations*. To be set apart as a monk, nun, or priest was to be called to a higher life, untainted by the inevitable compromises that came with living in a family, going to school, and working at a job. No wonder that Martin Luther would soon find himself at the entrance to a cloister, requesting permission to become a monk.

Luther as monk. Courtesy of Wikimedia Commons.

A Vocation at Last?

In 1505, Luther left law school and entered a monastery in Erfurt. This was a radical step for the young law student. It upset his father terribly because it meant a change in his own financial future. Why did he do it?

The story of Luther's call to become a monk has been interpreted in a number of ways. Most likely, he already had some misgivings about a career in law. But there was also a dramatic incident that he cited later in life. About a month after embarking on his legal studies in Erfurt, he was walking home (a three-day journey) and was caught in a frightening thunderstorm. A bolt of lightning came so close that it physically knocked him to the ground. Fearing for his life, he promised his patron protector, St. Ann, that he would become a monk. Surviving the storm, he now found himself with a genuine vocation, or so he thought.

There were many options for someone wishing to be a monk in sixteenth-century Europe. Monasteries were a prominent feature in Erfurt's landscape. Luther chose a fairly strict one that traced its tradition back to the famous fourth-century theologian, Augustine. As we saw in the previous chapter, a notable authority such as Thomas Aquinas viewed the entrance to holy orders as a "second baptism." Now able to dedicate himself fully to God, Luther began a life regulated by a careful schedule. He worshipped seven times a day, rising at 2:00 a.m. in the morning for the first service. He committed himself to a rigorous routine of self-examination, scouring his conscience for evidence that he had failed to live up to the demands of God's holy law. He wore rough, coarse clothing, ate and drank a minimal amount, and slept in an austere cell, fearful that any level of comfort would distract him from his true end. God and the church were also understood to be present in the sacraments. He would have regularly received the Eucharist. Eventually, he was ordained a priest, also a sacrament that conferred upon the ordinand an "indelible character" that gave him the power to consecrate the bread and wine and transform it into the very body and blood of Christ.

But, above all, it was the sacrament of penance that led Luther to question his calling. As noted in the last chapter, penance involved three separate aspects. First, a penitent had to confess his sins to a priest. The confession had to be done out of genuine love of God and not for any benefit that might be received. In other words, the intention behind the confession must be sorrow for sin because God's honor was violated, and not for ulterior motives such as avoiding the punishment of purgatory or hell. Furthermore, a confession had to be complete. Sins not confessed remained on the account of the penitent. So, it was important to recall your sins and equally valuable to have an alert and thorough confessor or you might leave the sacrament with an incomplete confession. The second step involved the absolution or forgiveness of sins by the confessor. The final stage of the sacrament led the penitent to make satisfaction for the sins committed. Here, a "penance" (five Hail Marys, ten Our Fathers) was assigned by the confessor to humble and discipline the sinner and awaken a desire to avoid infractions against God's law.

It was penance—the place of the church's most significant contact with the lives of people—where Luther was tripped up, and ultimately, led to question the whole understanding of vocation in the late medieval church. Luther had a scrupulous conscience, but not one that made him "crazy" or abnormal. He earnestly desired to live a pure life before God and he took the instructions of the church seriously. Notice, too, that grace was not absent in Luther's monastic experience. He regularly received the body and blood of Christ in Holy Communion. He heard the *te absolve* (In Christ's name you are forgiven your sins) from his confessor. But he also believed that he had to make an honest and sincere effort on his part in order to cooperate with the grace bestowed in the sacraments. And this is where things got complicated because Luther never felt he could do enough to merit the grace necessary to make himself right with God. As he puts it in his own words:

> When I was a monk, I made a great effort to live according to the requirements of the monastic rule. I made a practice of confessing and reciting all my sins, but always with prior contrition; I went to confession frequently, and I performed the assigned penances faithfully. Nevertheless, my conscience could never achieve certainty but was always in doubt and said: "You have not done this correctly. You were not contrite enough. You omitted this in your confession." Therefore the longer I tried to heal my uncertain, weak, and troubled conscience with human traditions, the more uncertain, weak, and troubled I continually made it.[2]

Ironically, Luther entered the monastery thinking that he had gained a true calling in life. But while living out his vocation as a monk, he found himself in the midst of a frightening spiritual descent. Instead of making progress in his goal of union with God, he was thrown into an abyss of darkness and despair. And the story of his recovery involved a slow and pain-filled path that ultimately led him to rethink the entire meaning of the word "vocation."

What happened next to Luther is nothing less than a conversion or a complete change of direction. But we must use the word "conversion" carefully because, for many, it means a

2. Martin Luther, "Commentary on Galatians" (1535) in *LW* 27:13.

one-time experience of great anguish where one finally gives oneself over to God. Luther would have gladly given himself over to God. The problem was his total inability to do this. He had to be liberated or freed by a power much greater than himself. He likened his situation to that of the dry earth in need of rain. The parched soil requires water, but it is completely unable to produce it on its own. Rather, it must wait for the blessing of a shower from above.[3] In a similar way, Luther says humanity is completely dependent upon God for release from its bondage.

Luther's liberation comes from a source he thought he knew well—the story of the death of Jesus of Nazareth. And it doesn't come all at once, but is more like the gradual light that spreads at dawn. Scholars have tried to pin down a precise time for the change, but have not had much success. For our purposes, it seems best to say that Luther's new understanding of God—and his new understanding of vocation—comes well after the momentous thunderstorm. It is deeply linked with his desire to study Scripture (he receives his doctorate in the Bible in 1512) and become a teacher. It is not even fully developed ten years after (1515) his entrance into the cloister in Erfurt. However, the new insight seems firmly in hand by the time he posts his 95 Theses in 1517 in protest of the sale of indulgences.

How did Luther's new view of God and earthly life come about? More than anything else, it is re-evaluation of the meaning of Christ's death on the cross. Up to this point, Luther accepted the commonly held view of Christ. Christians today are accustomed to seeing Christ as a savior. Though it may sound strange, that was not Luther's image of Jesus. Above all, Christ was viewed, as the Apostles' Creed puts it, as the one "coming to judge the living and the dead." For Luther,

3. Luther, *Commentary on Galatians* (1535) in LW 26:6.

that was a terrifying prospect. As a monk, he had pledged himself to the goal of perfection. This meant not only obeying the letter of the law, but also the spirit of the law. The latter becomes especially clear in Jesus' preaching of the Sermon on the Mount. Not only were his followers to avoid adultery, they were to refrain from lust as well (Matthew 5:21–22). Not only was killing forbidden, but so was hatred of a fellow human being (Matthew 5:27–28). And Christ's death? That was primarily an example of how to persevere in discipleship. In other words, righteousness was something he earned or achieved. Grace may have been in the picture, but it was mostly obscured by the demands of holiness.

The breakthrough occurs through an intensive study of the Bible and the gradual emergence of a new understanding of why Jesus died. Luther describes his new viewpoint in numerous places. Perhaps the most moving explanation from his early writings can be found in his treatise, *The Freedom of a Christian*, which he wrote in 1520. Here, he talks about how a union with God is actually achieved. It is not based on human merit or activity. Humanity is absolutely powerless to restore the relationship broken by its own rebellion. In fact, when it does try to earn salvation, it only falls into the sin of pride. In other words, trying to be "good" or "righteous" only makes things worse![4] But Christ, in his death, has initiated the "great exchange" that completely reverses the situation. Luther uses imagery drawn from a wedding to make his point. Christ takes on the role of bridegroom while a hostile or indifferent

---

4. "On the other hand, the self-righteous, who refrain from sins outwardly and seem to live blameless and religious lives, cannot avoid a presumption of confidence and righteousness, which cannot coexist with faith in Christ. Therefore, they are less fortunate than tax collectors or harlots, who do not offer their good works to a wrathful God in exchange for eternal life, as the self-righteous do, since they have none to offer, but beg that their sins be forgiven them for the sake of Christ." Luther, "Commentary on Galatians" (1535) in *LW* 27:14.

humanity becomes the bride. Christ's death brings about the exchange. Luther is really asking his readers to think about what happens at an actual wedding. In most circumstances, when the couple is pronounced "husband and wife," a significant change occurs—the property and obligations of each partner are transferred to the other person in the union. A groom's debt of $5,000 now becomes his wife's debt. Or a bride's car payment now becomes the groom's responsibility as well.

Just as a marriage results in a transfer of property (and liabilities), so Christ takes from his bride all her shame, rebellion, guilt, despair, and doubt. And he, in turn, bestows on her what she lacks—healing, forgiveness, life, and a good conscience. In other words, *in Christ*, the bride becomes righteous—the very goal she had sought and failed to obtain through her good works. This marriage costs Christ dearly, of course. This is not an equal or fair exchange. Rather, an unfathomable love compels him to take the bride's sin on his own literal body and it does what sin does well—it kills him. But because he is both human and divine, death will not get the last word. God raises him from the dead and promises the bride forgiveness and life, now and beyond the grave. Luther expresses it beautifully in *The Freedom of a Christian*:

> For Christ is God and man in one person. He has not sinned or died and he is not condemned. Nor can he sin, die, or be condemned. The righteousness, life, and salvation he possesses are unconquerable for he is eternal and all-powerful; however, by the wedding ring of faith, he shares in the sins, death and hell of his bride. In fact, he makes them his own and acts as if they were his own. It is as if he sinned, suffered, died, and descended into hell in order to overcome them all; however, sin, death, and hell could not swallow him. In fact, they were swallowed by him in a mighty duel or battle. For his righteousness is greater than all sin . . . thus the soul that trusts Christ and receives him as its

bridegroom through its pledge of faith is free from all sins, secure against death and hell, and given eternal righteousness, life and salvation.[5]

Thus, it is the cross of Christ that disrupts Luther's whole understanding of vocation. If our relationship to God is dependent wholly on what Christ has done for us, then the notion that we can lead some type of "holy" life to merit God's favor is radically undermined. The basis for a relationship with God is now trust (faith) in God's promises, and not in human performance. Or, it can be said in more theologically precise language: we are now justified (made right) with God by grace through faith and not human works. As might be expected, Luther's new insight will strike at the core of the entire monastic enterprise. Vocation is no longer the special province of monks and nuns.

A Genuine Vocation

Eventually, Luther would begin to doubt whether being a monk or nun was actually a God-ordained calling. But he did not leave the monastery immediately. Indeed, he was still wearing the black cowl of a monk when preaching in Wittenberg in the early part of the 1520s. But the break is now inevitable, and in 1521, he will write a treatise, *On Monastic Vows*, which virtually empties the monasteries in many regions of northern Germany.[6]

But now, we must consider the critical question of Luther's own vocation. The calling to be a monk in most cases is a false one since it is based on a desire to earn God's love and favor. In a letter to his father, written sixteen years after his

5. Martin Luther, *Freedom of a Christian*, trans. and introduced by Mark D. Tranvik (Minneapolis: Fortress Press, 2008), 62–63.
6. Brecht II:23–25.

own entrance into the monastery in Erfurt, he apologizes for disobeying Hans and admits his own vows to be worthless. He acknowledges that his father's suspicions about monastic life proved to be true and he ultimately thanks God for being the one to remove him from the cloister.[7]

What then was Luther's real vocation? For the answer to that, we must go back to his early years in the monastery, when he was selected from among his peers to be a student of theology. This allowed Luther to immerse himself in the history and theology of the church, and, most important, to study the Bible. In time, he would be transferred from Erfurt to the Augustinian monastery in Wittenberg where, as a teacher and a preacher, he would lead the German reformation. In 1512, he was awarded the doctor's cap as a professor of the Bible. Here, we come to the core of Luther's own calling: teacher and interpreter of Scripture. This is what gave him the insights to confront the reigning theologies of his day. Luther would regularly appeal to his office as a "sworn Doctor of the Holy Scripture" as the basis for his authority to interpret the Bible.[8]

The vocation to teach Scripture also provided him with the courage to confront corrupt church practices. In 1517, this intrepid professor of theology would question the practice of selling indulgences. In the next four years, he would oppose an array of the church's finest teachers in the name of his calling to teach and interpret Scripture faithfully. His vocation would eventually lead him to challenge the vicar of Christ on earth—the pope. By 1520, Rome had had enough of Luther and his calling. He was given the ultimate punishment: excommunication.

7. Martin Luther, "Letter to Hans Luther" (November 21, 1521) in *LW* 48:329–36.
8. Brecht I:127.

As we come to the end of this early period of Luther's life, we are struck by a remarkable irony. Luther entered monastic life in pursuit of the only vocation approved by the church of his day. However, he ends up rejecting the monk's life as a true calling, but in turn, receives a genuine vocation as a preacher, teacher, father, spouse, and citizen. In a way, Luther's own life has become a parable for the way God works in the world:

> My vow was not worth a fig. . . . In short, it was taken in accordance with the doctrines of men and superstition of hypocrites, none of which has God commanded. But behold how much good (that) God (whose mercies are without number and whose wisdom is without end) has made to come out of all these errors and sins![9]

---

9. Luther, "Letter to Hans Luther," *LW* 48:332–33.

3

Baptism and the Called Life

When Luther comes to speak of the *baptizatus sum* ["I am baptized"] his heart overflows, for here he finds, as nowhere else, the most essential character of the Gospel most perfectly expressed. Here is grace offered that is nothing but grace because it is absolutely free; that is not conditioned by any scheme of cooperation between humanity and God; that is not limited by any ethical conditions in humanity. Here God's faithfulness is proclaimed, a faithfulness that is not destroyed by our faithlessness.[1]

Baptism performs the "joyful exchange" through which a sinner receives the righteousness of Christ and Christ takes over his sins. . . .[2]

As we have seen in previous chapters, many prominent theologians in the Middle Ages likened the entrance into a

---

1. Adolf Köberle, *The Quest for Holiness: A Biblical, Historical, and Systematic Investigation*, trans. by John C. Mattes (Eugene, OR: Wipf and Stock, 2004), 63–64.
2. Heiko A. Oberman, *Luther. Man Between God and the Devil* (New Haven: Yale University Press, 1989), 227.

monastery as a second baptism. When Luther crossed the threshold into the cloister in Erfurt, he was admonished by the prior or leader of the community that he had committed himself to a life of self-denial: a meager diet, simple clothing, regular confession, worship by the canonical hours, and fervent prayer. Perhaps most important of all, the entrance ceremony ended with the ominous charge: "Not he who begins but he who perseveres to the end will be saved."[3]

Luther's liberation to a true vocation comes when he understands that God's love or favor cannot be earned or merited. Rather, Christ bestows God's forgiveness freely in his death on the cross—the place where the believer becomes the beneficiary of the "joyous exchange." The taking of monastic vows minimized the significance of his baptism. As he begins to question the validity of the vows, the sacrament also emerges in a new light. The personal importance of baptism for Luther can hardly be overstated. It is now, for him, the ongoing means by which God invades and interrupts his life with the Word of Christ's love and forgiveness. He understands baptism as a vow that God has made to him, which anchors his freedom in Christ and propels him into a life of vocation.[4]

The Forgotten Sacrament

The late medieval church seemed determined to diminish the meaning of baptism. As was noted in the first chapter, Christians in Luther's day understood the necessity for baptism. After all, Adam and Eve did not sin alone. Their disobedience was the tragedy of all humanity. As the first

---

3. Ibid., 127.
4. See Mark D. Tranvik, "Luther on Baptism" in *Harvesting Martin Luther's Reflections on Theology, Ethics and the Church*, ed. Timothy J. Wengert (Grand Rapids: Eerdmans, 2004), 23–37.

parents, their rebellion "infected"—from birth—all who would follow with the taint of the original sin. Baptism was needed to wash away the stain of this inheritance. It also made sense to baptize infants because death without the removal of original sin would mean no admittance to heaven—even for the newly born.

A problem arose for the church about sins committed after baptism. The sacrament might wash away original sin, but what happens when a person comes of "age" (understood as seven—the so-called age of reason) and offends God and neighbor? Another remedy was needed. The sacrament of penance becomes known as the "second plank after the shipwreck." The church father Jerome used this metaphor to underline that post-baptismal sin casts all of humanity out to sea, where it faces certain death unless rescued by the "plank" of penance.[5] Penance becomes the primary means by which God's forgiveness is communicated to the Christian. By confessing to a priest, hearing absolution, and doing a work of satisfaction, one is reconciled to God, and also, made "pure" for the reception of Christ's body and blood in the Eucharist.

Luther attacks the church's sacramental system in 1520 in a treatise called *The Babylonian Captivity of the Church.* In this work, he laments the way "there are scarcely any who call to mind their own baptism, and still fewer who glory in it; so many other ways have been discovered for remitting sins and getting to heaven."[6] The focus should not be on what we can do for God, as often occurred in the various steps of the sacrament of penance. Rather, the spotlight is on what God has done for us. And baptism now becomes the place *in time* where

---

5. Martin Luther, "The Babylonian Captivity of the Church" (1520), *LW* 36:61.
6. Ibid., 58.

God applies the benefits of Christ's death and resurrection to us:

> Baptism signifies two things—death and resurrection, that is, full and complete justification . . . this death and resurrection we call the new creation, regeneration, and spiritual birth. This should not be understood only allegorically as the death of sin and the life of grace, as many understand it, but as actual death and resurrection. For baptism is not a false sign.[7]

In other words, for Luther, baptism becomes the place of salvation. But here, we must be careful as well. Luther is not saying that the ritual of baptism (pouring water over the head of the one being baptized) is what reconciles us to God. Rather, it is Christ working through baptism that is key. For baptism comes attached to a promise from God: "He who believes and is baptized shall be saved" (Mark 16:16). God's promises have the power to create faith in the hearts of those who hear them. It is the promise inseparably connected to the water of baptism that brings about the trust that makes one right before God.

These are important points that are somewhat abstract and difficult to understand. Let's go over the central issue using different language. When I hear what God has done for me in Christ (made me the beneficiary of the great exchange), I have faith (or trust) in God. The content of the promise that creates my faith is that I am actually joined to the death and resurrection of Christ. His victory over sin and death becomes *my* triumph over sin and death. Instead of having to "save" myself (status, achievement, looks, etc.), I am now saved by the action of Christ—in reality, joined to Christ. This is "good news" that has power to change me or reorder my life and way of thinking. So, when Luther talks about baptism as that which

---

7. Ibid., 68.

saves, he means that Christ is acting through baptism to join the believer to himself.

There are questions that often arise at this point: Why bother with baptism? Is not the verbal promise sufficient? Why invest so much in the water, the physical sign?

The Misunderstood Sacrament

Though Luther's rebellion against Rome started the sixteenth-century Reformation, he was hardly alone in his protest. Following in his wake would be a host of individuals and groups, who thought Luther's teaching on the sacraments was weak on this very point. These protesters, often lumped together as the Radical Reformation (the spiritual cousins of today's Baptists, Amish, and Mennonites), thought the external sign (water, in the case of baptism) did not, in any way, convey the reality and benefits of Christ's crucifixion to the believer. Rather, baptism was a sign or pledge made by the believer that one had already committed oneself to Christ.

While Luther's early writings on baptism will emphasize the importance of faith against the ritualism of Rome, in the later portion of his career, he will counter the claims of those who minimized the significance of the sign. Luther's premise is that faith is fragile and susceptible to temptation. Belief is difficult in even the best of circumstances because it is virtually oiled into our bones that we must *do something* to merit God's love and favor:

> The question of justification is an elusive thing—not in itself, for in itself it is firm and sure, but so far as we are concerned. I myself have had considerable experience of this, for I know how I sometimes struggle in the hours of darkness. I know how often I suddenly lose sight of the rays of the Gospel and of grace, which have been obscured for me by thick, dark clouds. In other words,

> I know how slippery the footing is even for those who are mature and seem to be firmly established in matters of faith . . . (faith) is a very elusive matter because we are so unstable. In addition, we are opposed by half of ourselves, namely by reason and all its powers . . . This is why we continually teach that the knowledge of Christ and of faith is not a human work but utterly a divine gift; as God creates faith, so he preserves us in it.[8]

In 1528, he wrote an important treatise called *Concerning Rebaptism*, where he stresses the importance of the objective sign. This writing is basically a response to two pastors who wrote to Luther and asked for advice about how to handle people in their community who were denying the importance of baptism and stressing the need for faith. While Luther acknowledges the importance of faith, he is wary of a subjectivism that puts the focus on the self and its ability to believe, and not on Christ and the great exchange:

> True, one should add faith to baptism. But we are not to base baptism on faith. There is quite a difference between having faith, on the one hand, and depending one's faith and making baptism depend on faith, on the other. Whoever allows himself to be baptized on the strength of his faith, is not only uncertain, but also an idolator who denies Christ.[9]

8. Martin Luther, "Commentary on Galatians" (1535), *LW* 26:63–64.
9. Martin Luther, "Concerning Rebaptism" (1528), *LW* 40:252.

Melanchthon baptizes an infant. Courtesy
of Wikimedia Commons.

Luther utters some strong words here when he accuses his
opponents of falling into idolatry. It may seem ironic for
Martin Luther, faith's champion, to condemn those who are
calling for faith. But as the previous two quotes illustrate,
Luther recognizes that faith is both uncertain and unstable.

An external anchor is needed to prevent faith from drowning in the swamp of the subjective self. God, in his mercy, has commanded the church to baptize. The knowledge that, in our own personal history, we were grafted into Christ in our baptism provides great comfort. Otherwise, we fall into the trap of "justification by belief" or the tendency to measure our relationship to God by the quality of our faith. That is nothing but a counsel to despair, says Luther, because our faith is similar to "butter in the sunshine."[10]

It is not surprising that Luther can barely contain himself when speaking of the benefits of baptism. He recognized that our time on earth is often troubled and uncertain. As we look outside of ourselves, we recognize the fragility of life, an existence threatened by loss, loneliness, and finally, death. As we look within, we see a dizzying array of conflicting motives that, if we are honest, reveal an astonishing capability for self-regard. This is a situation from which we must be saved. And, as Luther puts it, God has provided a remedy. As he says in his *Large Catechism*, "No greater jewel, therefore, and adorn our body and soul than baptism, for through it we become completely holy and blessed, which no other kind of life and no work on earth can acquire."[11]

Baptized for Life

Baptism not only anchors the believer in Christ; it is also the sacrament of daily life. As we have noted, in the view of the late medieval church, baptism is replaced by penance. Though indispensable, it was quickly eclipsed by confession as the remedy for post-baptismal sin. As we said at the beginning of

---

10. Ibid.
11. Luther, "Large Catechism," in *BC*:462.

the chapter, a source for this way of thinking was the church father Jerome, who saw penance as the "second plank after the shipwreck," and who thereby inferred that the power of baptism is broken because of sin. Luther, who wanted to emphasize baptism's lifelong significance, turns this image on its head:

> The ship remains one, solid, and invincible; it will never be broken up into separate "planks." In it are carried all those who are brought to the harbor of salvation, for it is the truth of God giving us his promise in the sacraments. Of course, it often happens that many rashly leap overboard into the sea and perish; these are those who abandon faith in the promise and plunge into sin. But the ship itself remains intact and holds its course unimpaired. If any one is able somehow by grace to return to the ship, it is not on any plank, but on the solid ship itself that he is borne to life.[12]

Luther did not want baptism to be replaced by the sacrament of penance. By the end of his treatise, *The Babylonian Captivity of the Church* (which outlined his new understanding of the whole sacramental system), he combines the two. Penance now becomes a way of talking about baptism: ". . . penance . . . is nothing but a way and return to baptism."[13]

Consequently, baptism is no longer the sacrament of infancy or merely an "initiation rite" by which one enters the church. (The latter term, popular in many church circles today, is completely at odds with Luther's view of the sacrament.) Now, baptism is intertwined with the earthly life—the vocation—of the believer. As Luther says in his *Small Catechism*:

> What then is the significance of such a baptism with water? Answer: It signifies that the old creature in us with all sins and evil desires is to be drowned and die through daily contrition and

12. Luther, "Babylonian Captivity," *LW* 36:61.
13. Ibid., 124.

repentance, and on the other hand that daily a new person is to come forth and rise up to live before God in righteousness and purity forever.[14]

Or, he can say, "this whole life is nothing else than a spiritual baptism that does not cease until death."[15]

What is Luther's concern here? The emphasis on baptism's lifelong power and relevance is necessary because of sin. Although we are "pure and spotless" at the moment of baptism, sin continues to adhere to us. However, he wants to underline that sin's power does not have the final say. Since baptism is our "actual death," we are comforted to know the result of God's future judgment. While it is true that our physical bodies will eventually perish, the baptized know that the death which they should really fear—the death that would separate them from God—*has already occurred* in baptism. In our daily (or hourly!) return to our baptism, we have the assurance that God does not impute sins. That is, God does not hold our sin against us. Rather, God "winks" at them because of the pledge made in baptism.[16]

The Baptismal Edge: Luther's Own Calling

Up to this point, our discussion of baptism has focused on the assurance it provided Luther in his struggle with the monastic ideal and his battle against those who would minimize baptism in the name of "faith." We also underlined the importance of baptism as the sacrament that extends beyond infancy to the entire life of the believer. Most discussions of Luther's view stress these points alone. But something else needs to be highlighted. Baptism was not only a lifelong source of identity

---

14. Martin Luther, "The Small Catechism" (1528) in *BC*:360.
15. Martin Luther, "The Holy and Blessed Sacrament of Baptism" (1519), *LW* 35:30.
16. Ibid., 34.

and comfort for Luther. Because we are baptized into *Christ*—and his transforming love and grace—the sacrament sets things in motion. That is, it moves us beyond the status quo and often means a challenge to all that is comfortable and predictable.

There is no better witness to baptism's "edge," that is, its transformative power, than Luther's own life. As he lived out his vocation, he challenged virtually every convention of his age. Pope, church, prince—no authority was safe from his assaults. Dietrich Bonhoeffer, the Lutheran pastor martyred by the Nazis, had some perceptive remarks about Luther's vocation:

> Vocation in the New Testament sense is never a sanctioning of the worldly orders as such. Its Yes always includes at the same time the sharpest No, the sharpest protest against the world. Luther's return from the monastery into the world, into a "vocation," is, in the genuine spirit of the New Testament, the fiercest attack that has been launched and the hardest blow that has been struck against the world since the time of earliest Christianity . . . Luther's sole purpose in returning to the world was to be fully responsible to the call of Christ. In light of this call, the monastic solution remains wrong in two respects. First, it confines the ultimately responsible life to the space within the walls of the monastery. Second, it regards as only a false compromise the life in which the Yes and the No to living in this world—both of which are included in the call of Jesus Christ—are to be united in concrete responsibility to this call.[17]

As we have seen, Luther no longer considered monasticism to be a genuine calling, save for a few who, by a miracle of God, were able to uphold the discipline of the cloister without thinking that it elevated them in the eyes of God. As a teacher

---

17. Dietrich Bonhoeffer, *Ethics*, trans. by Reinhard Krauss, Charles C. West, and Douglas W. Stott (Minneapolis: Fortress Press, 2009), 291–92.

and preacher, he now grounds his identity in his baptism. As
he puts it in his *Large Catechism*:

> Thus, we must regard baptism and put it to use in such a way
> that we may draw strength and comfort from it when our sins or
> conscience oppress us, and say: "But I am baptized! And if I have
> been baptized, I have the promise that I shall be saved and have
> eternal life, both in soul and body."[18]

One sees this movement toward baptism most clearly in his
reassessment of the call to a religious order. Again, it is
important to keep in mind the significance of what Luther
was doing when he adopted the cowl of a monk. It meant a
complete break with his previous life. A man was not allowed
to enter a monastery with personal property, so Luther gave
away all his possessions—whatever money he had as well as
his clothes and his books. Moreover, he agreed to forfeit any
dreams of having a wife and children. His new life was to be
chaste in body and soul. Finally, he pledged obedience to the
abbot of the monastery, who would have almost total control
of his comings and goings. Most important of all, Luther was
making a pledge to almighty God that his life would now be in
total service to him.

When Luther rejects monastic vows, he does so in the name
of another vow—one that God has made to him in baptism. He
laments the confusion that has resulted from monasticism—it
has caused monks and nuns to place their loyalties where they
do not belong and forget their true foundation in the Christian
life:

> They (monks and nuns) are no longer called Christians or
> children of God, but rather Benedictines, Dominicians,
> Franciscans, Augustinians. They boast of these names and of

---

18. Luther, "The Large Catechism," *BC*:462.

their father-founders more than they do of Christ . . . they think that keeping the rules of their order is essential for righteousness and salvation . . . by trusting in these things, pursuing their own interests, and expecting to be crowned before God because they were monks, they have forgotten they have been baptized into the works of Christ[19]

Moreover, Luther asserts the false call to a monastic life causes those in holy orders to reject the greatest commandment of all: love of neighbor.[20] Leaving the world in the name of achieving one's own personal salvation is contrary to what God intended for creation. Much better (and holier!) to be a husband, wife, family member, and servant and live in the world in service of the neighbor than to search for a realm where one might seek a selfish purity.[21]

Luther's rejection of monastic vows and his new calling as a teacher and preacher moves him into a world of other vocations as well. As we shall see, there is a renewal of his call to be a son to his parents. And though he was reluctant at first to get married (he expected his own imminent death and thought it would be irresponsible to burden a wife and family with such a loss), he eventually weds and becomes a father to six children. Additionally, given the prominent role he will play in the politics of the sixteenth century, he discovers many new dimensions of what it means to be called to be a citizen. All of these remarkable changes can be traced at a certain level to Luther's rediscovery of the importance of baptism and the corresponding diminishment of the vocation of the monk.

The second part of this work will focus on the areas or arenas to which a Christian is called. But we will not be leaving Luther's story behind. Each section will continue to draw on

19. Martin Luther, "The Judgment of Martin Luther on Monastic Vows" (1521), LW 44:363.
20. Martin Luther, "Confession Concerning Christ's Supper" (1528), LW 37:362–65.
21. Luther, "Monastic Vows," LW 44:363.

the Reformer's calling in these spheres. In addition, we will mimic Luther's ongoing concern that theology be made relevant to people. This can be seen in his *Small Catechism*, written to explain the basics of the faith to the ordinary Christian. At the conclusion of each section, Luther inserts the question, "What Does This Mean?" We will follow a similar method in the upcoming chapters.

PART II

The Called Life

4

It Gets Personal

God calls . . . me. It is not selfish or self-centered to affirm the profoundly personal dimension of vocation. . . . Against the generic ideal of monastic life, Luther argued that Christ calls each of us to serve God and neighbor where we are, as we are. It is a specific person, not a state of life that Christ addresses. The plan that is divine providence stretches out across all of human history, touching billions of individuals—each with his or her own history and complex psychology, each with a story that is unique. To speak of the God who calls without at the same time attending to the person who hears this call is to distort the divine-human dialogue. It misses something central to vocation.[1]

Following his dramatic testimony at the Diet of Worms in 1521, Martin Luther was "kidnapped" by his prince and brought to his imposing Wartburg Castle in Eisenach, Germany. This was for Luther's own protection, and also to allow the tense stand-off between the reformer and Rome to cool down. Save for

---

1. Edward Hahnenberg, *Awakening Vocation: A Theology of Christian Call* (Collegeville, MN: Liturgical Press, 2010), 125.

63

one brief visit to Wittenberg in disguise, Luther remained at the Wartburg for nine months. During this time of enforced solitude, he exercised his calling as a teacher and preacher. Most famously, Luther translated the New Testament from Greek into German so that the literate people could read the Bible for themselves. He also wrote "model sermons" on biblical texts to assist other pastors who were leading the fragile reform movement.

However, in 1522, Luther feels called to end his imprisonment. He receives word from Wittenberg that some of the city and church leaders were moving too quickly and disturbing the consciences of the faithful. Pastors were getting married, images in churches were being destroyed, and Holy Communion was being distributed in both kinds. None of this was essentially against what Luther had been advocating, though he was not generally in favor of destroying images. But it was happening too fast. Disorder and confusion reigned in the city. Luther felt strongly that people needed to be educated before embarking on wholesale changes in church practice.

Luther's return to Wittenberg was risky, and not just for him. As a condemned heretic, he was under the ban of the empire. This also meant peril for anyone who publicly aided him. The prince of Electoral Saxony, Frederick the Wise, once again demonstrated great courage in allowing his condemned theology professor to publicly teach and preach. But most notable is what Luther said when he returned to Wittenberg.

He is scheduled immediately to give eight sermons in the city church. There is turmoil and agitation in the air. But Luther does not begin his preaching by scolding or threatening his listeners. Instead, he says the following:

> The summons of death comes to us all, and no one can die for another. Everyone must fight his own battle with death by

himself, alone. We can shout into another's ears, but everyone must himself be prepared for the time of death, for I will not be with you then, nor you with me. Therefore, everyone must know and be armed with the chief things that concern a Christian.[2]

Luther's rhetoric is intensely personal. In the midst of Wittenberg's unrest, he makes a solemn call for a sense of perspective. It is a "momento mori" moment, which is a Latin phrase meaning "remember you are to die." In other words, what is important right now for his listeners is that they recall who they are, and especially, the indisputable fact that, one day, their time on earth will cease and they will be called to account before God.

The sermon will go on to remind the people of Wittenberg of their calling in this situation. Luther cautions them about the need for patience with those upset over the changes. He counsels a faith active in love of neighbor—a love that keeps in mind not just what is allowed, but what is best for the community. But for our purposes, it is important to note where he begins. A sense of calling begins not with a consideration of the surrounding circumstances, but rather, with a laser-like focus on the self standing before God.

The Call is Personal

When discussing the personal dimension of vocation with reference to Luther, some words of caution are in order. Two concerns need to be addressed. The first is the tendency of some modern historians to see Luther as the herald of modern individualism. Often pointing to Luther's daring words at the Diet of Worms ("Here I stand, I can do no other"), he is cited as an early of example of the individual breaking free of the

2. Martin Luther, "The First Invocavit Sermon" (1522), *LW* 51:70.

church-state monolith of the Middle Ages. Luther becomes the first "modern man," a precursor of the Enlightenment's emphasis on individual autonomy. But Luther was hardly arguing for self-sufficiency, as it would be understood in the eighteenth century. In his speech at Worms, he stressed to his audience that his conscience was "captive to the Word of God." In other words, Luther was not standing up for the truth as determined by his own best lights. His protest rested on a deep engagement with Scripture and a long tradition of biblical interpretation. In his mind, the self is never "alone" and certainly not "autonomous," but rather, standing under the authority of God's Word.

A second concern is to warn against seeing Luther's views on vocation through the lens of the modern preoccupation with the self. Philip Rieff's *The Triumph of the Therapeutic* is a significant discussion of this phenomenon. According to Rieff, there are three ages in Western history. The first is the age of the "political man," as represented by the Greeks and their concern for the well-being of the *polis*. The second is the Christian period and its concern with the relationship between God and the soul. And the present age is one Rieff calls that of the "psychological man." Having banished God, we are left with the SELF. The inevitable consequence can be seen in our present culture and its incessant desire for personal peace and happiness. Organized religion has jumped on this bandwagon to the point where it is commonly accepted that faith is not an end in itself, but a means to feeling good about oneself. As Rieff memorably put it: "Religious man was born to be saved; psychological man is born to be pleased. . . ."[3]

Having registered these important caveats, it is important to

---

3. Phillip Rieff, *The Triumph of the Therapeutic: The Uses of Faith after Freud* (New York: Harper and Row, 1966), 19.

underline that Luther's understanding of vocation does begin with the individual, but not in the modern matrix of self-concern. A good example can be found in *The Freedom of a Christian*. As noted earlier, Luther wrote this treatise in 1520, shortly before he was excommunicated by Rome. His concern was to provide an overview of his teaching for what he called the "common" people. He felt his views were being distorted by his enemies and even misunderstood by some of his allies. So, he wanted to compose a work that summarized his teaching in simple language that could be understood by his growing audience of readers. The essay is divided into two parts. The first part discusses how Christ frees a Christian (with a substantial discussion of the joyous exchange). In the second half of the work, Luther talks about how Christian liberty leads to being bound to the needs of the neighbor. Except, he does not start with the neighbor—he starts with the *self*, and then, proceeds to a discussion of how our good works are to benefit others. Luther's interpreters often neglect this crucial point. While the neighbor is always the goal of Christian love, that love must first pass through the crucible of the self.[4]

This theme will be underlined throughout Luther's works. Perhaps its most famous expression comes in *The Small Catechism*, written in 1529 in order to nurture the faith and life of pastors and congregational members. Luther and his circle of reformers were wary of faith that rested only on the "facts" of the Bible. They dismissed this as a *fides historica* or "historical faith" that remained in the mind and did not sink down to the level of the heart.[5] For example, when discussing the Apostles' Creed and the belief in the "first article" (I believe

4. Luther, "Freedom of a Christian," 71–79.
5. See the comments of Luther's colleague, Philip Melanchthon, in his "Apology of the Augsburg Confession," in BC:128.

in God the Father almighty, creator of heaven and earth), he uses the following language:

> I believe that God has created *me* together with all that exists. God has given *me* and still preserves *my* body and soul. . . . God protects *me* from all danger and shields and preserves *me* from all evil. . . .[6]

Luther certainly wants Christians to know the content of the creed. But he also realizes that creedal language can be abstract and lifeless. It is important for the believer to know how he or she connects personally with this statement of faith. God doesn't just create in general—God has created all that exists and, most importantly, God has created *me*.

So, we have established for Luther the importance of the individual. God's call does not come in general, but to living human beings, each in his or her own particular circumstance. Given this emphasis on the individual in Luther's thinking, what does this practically mean for understanding his views on vocation?

Called to Die

I realize the title of this section sounds rather ominous. But if we use Luther and his views on baptism as our point of reference for thinking about vocation, then it makes a lot of sense. As mentioned above, Luther's first words to his congregation upon his return to Wittenberg from the Wartburg Castle were a reminder that, someday, they will die. He was referring here, of course, to the physical death that faces everyone. But he also stressed in many places that, in baptism, we are called to a daily (hourly?) death that is usually

---

6. Luther, "The Small Catechism," BC:354 (italics mine).

defined as repentance. The rhythm of the individual Christian life involves a regular acknowledgment of our own desire to seize control and confine God to a marginal role in our lives. The result is that we twist and distort our relationships with others. We end up conforming to what the Apostle Paul called the "spirit of this world" (I Cor. 2:12).

Luther recognized this in *The Freedom of a Christian*. He saw our freedom in Christ being threatened by our tendency to look to activities and objects outside ourselves as validation of our status. In his day, that meant becoming a monk or priest (the "real" vocations) or praying and fasting to impress God with our works. In our time, it might mean achieving a certain level of income or acquiring a degree or living in a certain neighborhood or wearing a fashionable type of clothing. Whatever the activity, when we trust something other than God for our true identity, we are "living outside in." In other words, something "out there" that is not God defines who we are, in the most fundamental sense. The result, says Luther, is that God is not honored and we end up living in bondage to whatever "gods" we have entrusted our lives. And because these "gods" are incapable of either forgiving us or insuring that death does not have the last word, a certain restlessness or anxiety plagues those trapped by their false faith. Note that this predicament is not only the lot of those outside the Christian faith. It also describes every Christian. For Christians, too, regularly "fall" out of faith (trust something other than God).

For Luther, this baptismal death was not abstract. He connected it directly to the vocation of the Christian. In other words, he wants baptism to be grounded in confession and absolution. When we confess our sins, we "die" to sin, and when we hear the word of absolution or forgiveness, we are raised up to new life. Noteworthy is how Luther connects the calling of the Christian with confession. Listen to his counsel to those seeking to acknowledge their sin:

> Here reflect on your walk of life in light of the Ten Commandments: whether you are father, mother, son, daughter, master, mistress, servant; whether you have been disobedient, unfaithful, lazy, whether you have harmed anyone by word or deed, whether you have stolen, neglected, wasted or injured anything.[7]

Luther is not interested in a "general" confession that remains aloof from real life. Rather, our baptismal dying to self takes place within the home and workplace. The call to die then is the first movement of the individual's life of vocation. But it doesn't stop there. For at the center of the Christian story is the empty tomb.

Called to Life

Luther also reminds his readers in *The Small Catechism* that "daily a new person is to come forth and rise up to live before God in righteousness and purity forever."[8] As the empty tomb follows the cross, so repentance and death are followed by forgiveness and new life. Again, we must be careful of abstractions. The rhythm of the called life is an enemy of abstractions. In other words, the one called is raised from death to *life*, and not just life in general, but to the real and actual world of vocation. One is raised up as a daughter, son, mother, father, student, worker, or citizen. Standing on the other side of death, there is a decisive difference.

The world of creation is actually the world of vocation. The

---

7. Luther, "The Small Catechism," *BC*:360.
8. Ibid.

one called now lives within her vocation in order that the neighbor might be served. No longer does she seek to live "outside in" and have the values and standards of the world determine her identity. She has been raised up or freed in the joyful exchange to live "inside out." The purpose of life is not self-fulfillment, but self-emptying on the model of Christ (Philippians 2:5-1).

Most monks and nuns in Luther's day had a false calling because they were seeking to escape regular life and earn salvation by means of their pious works. For Luther, the new "holy orders" are found in the congregation, the home (which included work in his view), and the government. And above these callings, he says, stands

> . . . the common order of Christian love, in which one serves not only the three orders (congregation, home and government) but also serves every needy person in general with all kinds of benevolent deeds, such as feeding the hungry, giving drink to the thirsty, forgiving enemies, praying for all men on earth suffering all kinds of evil on earth, etc. Behold, all of these are called good and holy works.[9]

As the Swedish scholar Gustaf Wingren summarized Luther's views: God does not need your good works. God is doing fine without them. But take a look around—your neighbor needs them. Indeed, the baptized one is raised to new life—a new life that takes place in God's good creation. He or she is returned to God's world to love and serve the neighbor.[10]

A Costly Call

When faith goes forth into the world in the form of love, it

9. Luther, "Confession Concerning Christ's Supper" (1528), *LW* 37:365.
10. Wingren, *Luther on Vocation*, 54–55. See also Robert Kolb, *Martin Luther: Confessor of the Faith* (New York: Oxford University Press, 2009), 172–73.

immediately meets resistance. As Luther reminded his readers in *The Small Catechism*, the baptismal death occurs daily. And it can take many forms. This death is not only the fruit of reflection on the commandments and our recognition of our desire to put something other than God at the center of our lives. The death occurs not only in devotions or reflection, but also in living out the Christian life. As we seek to serve the neighbor, we often end up suffering. Luther says this should not surprise us. In fact, we should expect that what happened to Christ should happen to us as well:

> . . . what happened historically and temporally when Christ came—namely he abrogated the Law and brought liberty and eternal life to light—this happens personally and spiritually every day in any Christian, in whom there are found the time of Law and the time of Grace in constant alteration.[11]

A similar thing can be seen in *The Freedom of a Christian*. As we seek to serve the neighbor in love, we actually repeat the joyous exchange that Christ enacted on our behalf.

> This teaching tells us that the good we have from God should flow from one to the other and be common to all. Everyone should "put on" the neighbor and act toward him or her as if we were in the neighbor's place. The good that flowed from Christ flows into us. . . . The good we receive from Christ flows from us toward those who have need of it. As a result, I should lay before God my faith and righteousness so that they may cover and intercede for the sins of my neighbor. I take these sins upon myself, and labor and serve in them, as if they were my very own. This is exactly what Christ did for us. This is true and sincere love and the rule of a Christian life.[12]

---

11. Martin Luther, "Lectures on Galatians" (1535), *LW* 26:340.
12. Luther, "Freedom of a Christian," 88.

van Gogh's *Good Samaritan*. Courtesy of Wikimedia Commons.

Perhaps another way to say this is that the Christian is driven to go where the pain is. We do not seek out pain as a way to gain favor with God. But if we live faithfully within our callings, we will find many occasions where love is needed. After all, Christ was one who crossed boundaries. Cultural and religious taboos were often broken as he reached out to the sick, the whores, and the tax collectors. As those whose

73

identity is yoked to Christ, we also go to the "hard" places because, like water seeking the lowest places, we also find ourselves driven by the Spirit to be with the hurting, the excluded, and the ostracized. And here, we meet the very face of Christ, as promised in Matthew 25:31-46. We do not bring Christ to the world so much as we meet Christ in the world.

This is difficult. Taking on the burdens of others, as modeled by Christ in the joyous exchange, leads to the cross. The term "cross" should be associated not just with physical suffering and pain (though, of course, it is that), but it also represents a frightful level of shame, loneliness, and rejection. Luther's calling in life led him to experience long and dark moments of despair. These desperate battles with temptation (he saw it as the work of Satan) plagued him his whole life. They even became more intense once he discovered his vocation as a teacher and preacher.

Over the course of his life, Luther turned more and more to baptism as the best remedy against the doubt and darkness that threatened his sense of calling.[13] Luther had a remarkable ability to identify deeply with the texts of the Bible. Luther did not just "read" Scripture. Rather, he meditated on it, which means, in part, that he read his own life and circumstances into the biblical story.[14] The text was personal and never just an account that happened centuries earlier. The importance of baptism as a grounding for Luther's faith can be seen vividly in a writing from late in his career—the story of Abraham's order to sacrifice his son, Isaac.

The book of Genesis might seem to be an unlikely place to reflect on baptism.[15] After all, it takes place at the start of the

---

13. See Kolb, *Confessor*, 135–41.
14. See Kolb, *Stories of God*, for an extended discussion of how Luther saw his life and that of his listeners and readers intertwined with the biblical text.

Old Testament, long before any baptisms are recorded in the Bible. But Luther saw his own struggle for faith in the horrific command of God to Abraham in Genesis 22:1–14 to sacrifice his beloved son Isaac, the child of the promise. Luther says Abraham faced a horrible contradiction, at least according to the standards of human reason: "If Isaac must be killed, the promise is void; but if the promise is sure, it is impossible that this is a command of God."[16] He marvels at Abraham's faith in the face of this paradox. But he also knows that living out a calling often leads to shadowy places of temptation, confusion, and despair. And the only remedy is to hold God to his promises. At three different points in this remarkable section of the commentary, Luther lifts up baptism as the anchor needed in the midst of desperation and despair:

> This trial (of Abraham) cannot be overcome and is far too great to be understood by us. For there is a contradiction with which God contradicts himself. It is impossible for flesh to understand this; for it inevitably concludes either that God is lying—and this is blasphemy—or that God hates me—and this leads to despair.... We are frequently tempted by thoughts of despair; for what human being is there who could be without this thought: "What if God did not want you to be saved?" But we are taught in the conflict we must hold fast to the promise given us in Baptism, which is sure and clear.[17]

A few paragraphs later, Luther will reflect that the strange call to sacrifice Isaac was written for our comfort so that "we may learn to rely on the promises we have. I was baptized. Therefore I must maintain that I was translated from the kingdom of Satan into the kingdom of God." Moreover, says Luther, the Devil attacks with a special intensity those who

---

15. Jonathan Trigg, *Baptism in the Theology of Martin Luther* (New York: Brill, 1994) shows how baptism permeates his lectures on Genesis.
16. Martin Luther, "Lectures on Genesis" (1538), *LW* 4:93.
17. Ibid.

trust in Christ's righteousness alone for their identity. Here, the only remedy is baptism, which is where one is united to Christ and promised his grace.[18]

It might be helpful to summarize the contents of this chapter. We began by highlighting the importance of the individual (though not in an autonomous sense) in thinking about what it means to have a vocation. Using *The Freedom of a Christian* and *The Small Catechism* as guides, we stressed how the self is the starting point for the called life. We also suggested that vocation can be understood within the structure of baptism and that it consists of three movements: we are called to die, we are called to life, and the call is costly. Now, we move to the next section, what can be called "practical theology." Following the rhythm of Luther's catechism (and the question 'What does this mean?'), we ask about the implications of this teaching for Christians and congregational life.

What Does This Mean?

The title of this chapter is "It Gets Personal." The suggestion here is not to argue for a focus on the self, but rather, to stress the importance of a personal dimension when thinking about what it means to have a called life. A sense of calling emerges when we view ourselves as liberated children of God, blessed with particular gifts, which we then are to use in service to our communities.

If I had to make one compelling argument for what it means to be a Christian, I would underline the gift of freedom. Many associate "religion" with a system of laws and rules. In other words, it all boils down to controlling behavior and keeping people in line. Others view faith as merely a preparation for

18. Ibid., 94–95.

a future life after death. The connection to here and now is faint or secondary. Paul and Luther begin in a different place. Paul reminds the Galatians "for freedom Christ has set us free" (Galatians 5:1). And when Luther summarizes the gospel, he speaks of how a "Christian is Lord of all, completely free of everything."[19]

At the heart of Luther's *Small Catechism* is his explanation of the second article of the Apostles' Creed. He is unpacking the meaning of Jesus Christ for his readers:

> He has redeemed me, a lost and condemned human being. He has purchased and freed me from all sins, from death, and from the power of the devil, not with silver and gold but with his holy, precious blood and with his innocent suffering and death. He has done all this in order that I many belong to him, live under him in his kingdom, and serve him in eternal righteousness, innocence and blessedness, just as he is risen from the dead and lives and rules eternally.[20]

Luther is trying to make the case that the gift of Christian freedom is closely connected to the gift of time.

Think of how difficult it is for us to live in the present. When things are not going well for us, we tend to be either lost in the past or worried about the future. We are literally "captured" or bound by things we have done (or by things that have been done to us). Alternatively, we are hemmed in by worries about the future. Sometimes, our thoughts about the future have a definite shape as, for example, when we are waiting for the results of an important medical test. Often, our dread of the future is not clear. It is a general sense of anxiety, often not well-defined, about something "bad" that might happen. In either case, the past or the future command our attention and

---

19. Luther, "Freedom of a Christian," 50.
20. Luther, "The Small Catechism," in BC:355.

keep us from the present. When that happens, we cease to be grateful for life and we are also less attentive to the needs of others because we are so wrapped up in our own issues.

For Luther, Christ provides us with the freedom to live, that is, to be fully present. The language is traditional, but actually packed with great power: "He has purchased and freed me from all sins, from death, and from the power of the devil. . . ." In other words, Christ has released us from an "imprisonment"—our tendency to either dwell on the past or be anxious about the future.

With regard to what has happened, the promise is complete forgiveness. This does not erase the past, but rather, disarms it. What *has happened* no longer has the power to control us. It is something like getting the tires aligned on your car. Now, it steers straight. You are no longer hampered by the need to always correct for the flaw in the alignment. Furthermore, the force that threatens to make life meaningless—death—has been robbed of its power. Christ's victory over death means a life marked by hope rather than fear.

Note, too, that Luther mixes in talk of Satan with his comments about sin and death. Language about the devil might strike us as quaint or old-fashioned, but Luther took seriously a force in the world that opposed Christ and made it difficult to know true life in the present. This force, named the devil by Luther and the Scriptures, is the true menace behind sin and death. Luther believes the devil uses both our regrets and fears to keep us from living in the present. As a result, we tend to become self-absorbed, and, most important, we lose the gift of the present moment. Life loses its joy as we become less grateful. And our obscured vision means the needs of the neighbor are no longer clearly in view. Sin and death, stirred up by the considerable power of the devil, twist our lives into shapes never intended by our good Creator.

Living a called life means recognizing, first of all, that this ongoing struggle with the past, the future, and the powers of darkness is a battle that every person must face daily. There is no evading it. Trust in God is fragile, and at times, elusive. By God's grace, the gift of the present (which is the abundant life in Christ mentioned in John 10:10) must be reclaimed on a daily and even hourly basis. While this is not the place to present a full program for how this might be done, we do have clues from Luther's own vocation about some things that might be done.

First, keep baptism front and center, both in private devotion, and also, in the worship life of the church. Faith is the result of our union with the crucified and risen Christ. For Luther, baptism—our daily dying and rising with Christ—had an ongoing vitality in the life of the Christian. It was the power that kept him fully alive and living in the present. Not surprisingly, he regularly crossed himself in remembrance of his baptism.

Living a called life demands a baptismal foundation. The very first word of our day should not be something on a long list of tasks, but rather, a thankful remembrance of our baptismal identity as a child of God. Only then do we embark on our various callings. And living out our vocations from within a baptismal framework means that we will meet Christ in the needs of the neighbor. It might be a daughter who needs help with homework before breakfast or a neighbor who needs a ride to school. It might be a failing school that requires attention. Or it might come in the form of a webpage headline announcing a tragic earthquake that has caused thousands to be without adequate food or shelter. But one thing is certain: the called life means that Christ will come to you. He will be hidden behind all types of faces and situations. But Christ will not leave you alone. And you will return again and again to your baptism and its rhythm of death and life as you tend to your vocation. Finally, the last word of the day is also baptismal. As you close your eyes, the focus in not on what you accomplished or failed to do, but rather, a sense of gratitude that God's love for you in Christ is the final word to be heard.

Given baptism's centrality, a called life also needs the sacrament to be front and center in the worship life of the church. Too often, baptism is treated as the "second sacrament" behind the Lord's Supper. But, with some imagination and commitment, it is possible to restore baptism to its central place.

Some years ago, I worshipped in a church in Germany that did just that. A large baptismal font, capable of submerging an adult, was in the center of the sanctuary. The water bubbled with life and the green plants surrounding the font made clear that water actually *gave* life. A lit Christ candle helped to illumine the space. I noticed that people entering the church made their way to the font, dipped their hand in the water, and then crossed themselves. The actual service itself began at the font with a brief order of confession and forgiveness. As the pastor spoke the words of absolution, her hand was wet with what Luther called "the gracious water of life."

Later in the service, a young boy, maybe ten years old, was baptized. But the pastor made clear that this was not something just happening to the boy, but rather, an occasion for the entire community to remember their own baptisms. Rather than being passive "observers" of the baptismal service, the pastor's words and the liturgy used underlined that Christ was coming to each of us in that service, and that not one, but a hundred baptisms were being celebrated that morning.

Living a called life is not easy. We are in a culture that subverts faith at every turn, tempting us to think that our identity is based on the performance principle or our ability to achieve goals that are fundamentally self-centered. Consequently, faith needs an anchor in order to thrive. Baptism in Christ provides that foundation. It grounds us in the freedom of faith and makes us fully alive in the present. And it propels us out into God's world in our vocations in service of the neighbor.

Questions for Discussion

1. If you have been baptized, how often do you recall it and reflect on its meaning? Why does it seem to be so difficult to keep baptism central in our individual lives and in our communities of faith?

2. What is it about Luther's call to "die" that is really life-giving? How do think about this in your own life and sense of vocation?

3. When stressing the personal dimension of vocation, I often have my students talk about "interruptions" that have happened in their lives. Think of Moses, David, the apostle Paul or Mary, the mother of Jesus. The Bible is full of people whose calls were shaped by interruptions. We often see our lives moving on a certain path, only to have an interruption (illness, conversation, argument, book, job loss, a moment of inspiration, etc.) set us in a different direction. Reflecting on interruptions can be a good way to think about the way that God is involved in our lives. Discuss the interruptions in your life and how they have shaped your sense of calling.

5

The Call to Be a Son, Spouse, and Father

"I am the son of a peasant . . . and the grandson and the great grandson. My father wanted to make me into a burgomaster [mayor]. He went to Mansfeld and became a miner. I became a baccalaureate and a master..Then I became a monk and put off the brown beret. My father didn't like it, and then I got into the pope's hair and married an apostate nun. Who could have read that in the stars?"[1]

We now move to the domestic realm in our look at the called life. We continue to use Luther's vocation as our guide, but we immediately run into some problems of definition. As noted earlier, in Luther's day, there were three distinct spheres where a calling was lived out: the domestic, civil, and ecclesiastical realms. In the sixteenth century, the domestic jurisdiction included the roles of marriage, family, and work. In

---

1. Martin Luther, "Table Talk," *TR* 5:558 as quoted in Roland Bainton, *Here I Stand. A Life of Martin Luther* (Nashville: Abingdon, 1950), 231.

our rendering, however, we are restricting the domestic realm to marriage and family. Work will be in a separate category. The categories themselves are not important. What is crucial is the recovery of Luther's insight that God calls us in every area of our creaturely life and not just in supposedly "sacred" or "religious" moments.

When we look at Luther's relationship with his parents, and later, his own family life, it is apparent that volumes can be written about these topics. The purpose of this study is not to go into exhaustive detail about these relationships, but rather, get glimpses of key moments when Luther lived out his calling as a son, spouse, and parent. The hope is that these brief glances will provide insights for how we can think about our own vocation in each of these spheres.

Luther's parents. Courtesy of Wikimedia Commons.

Luther the Son

Vocation figures prominently in Luther's relationship with his mother and his father. In many biographies, his mother is hardly mentioned. And it is true that information about

Margaret Luther is hard to come by. But it is now clear that, unlike his father Hans, she did not come from a peasant background. Her family was well-established in the German city of Eisenach, where later, Luther would spend nine months as a fugitive in the Wartburg Castle. Moreover, members of her family served on town councils, received university educations, and practiced law and medicine. People have long puzzled how Luther could have received his education when his father was simply a copper miner. The answer now seems clear: on his mother's side, there was a tradition of study at a university. It now appears that Luther's extensive schooling (which would have been rare for a peasant) was made possible by his mother.[2] Margaret Luther may be obscure, but we know enough to say that she enabled her son to pursue an education, and eventually, his calling as preacher and theologian.

Much more ink has been spilled discussing Luther's relationship with his father. While much of the attempt to psychologize Luther relationship with Hans Luther has been rightly questioned, it is clear that the connection between the father and son was frayed and complicated, but ultimately reconciled.[3] In short, it was messy. Above all, two letters from son to father provide us with a lens that allows a look at some of the dynamics.

The first letter was written in 1521 from the Wartburg castle, which, as we have seen, was a time of turmoil in Wittenberg. A spirit of rebellion was in air. Monks and nuns were not only breaking their vows—they were also getting married. Luther put the letter to his father as an introduction to his powerful

---

2. Oberman, *Between God and Devil*, 85–91.

3. The classic work that analyzed Luther's relationship with his father is Erik Erickson's *Young Man Luther: A Study in Psychoanalysis and History* (New York: Norton, 1958). The problems with this approach are discussed in a series of essays found in *Psychohistory and Religion: The Case of Young Man Luther*, ed. by Robert Johnson (Philadelphia; Fortress Press, 1977).

treatise, *The Judgment on Monastic Vows*, which became a key factor in the dissolution of monasteries and nunneries in the areas where the Lutheran movement was taking hold. It can be read as Luther's personal explanation to his father for the dramatic change in his calling. It also served as an example to those contemplating a similar alteration in their vocations.

Like in our time, the desires and wishes of parents complicate the decisions surrounding vocation. As we have seen, Hans Luther was shaped by his work as a miner. He knew well the risks and hard work involved in extracting copper from an unforgiving earth. He clearly wanted something different for his own son. Our quote at the beginning of the chapter suggests that he envisioned Martin as the mayor of a town or city. In the letter itself, Luther also says his father wished for him an "honorable and wealthy marriage." The message from the father is clear: "I want a life for you that I never was able to have. I want for you to be well-regarded as a citizen and also the material prosperity that my own family never enjoyed. I also want for you a family and children." Attendant to all these desires, of course, is the reasonable hope that Martin himself might assist his parents as they aged and were no longer able to work.[4]

But Luther did something that temporarily shattered the relationship between father and son: he left the study of law and entered a monastery "without the knowledge and against the will" of Hans. This must have really stung. Note what is being said here. He not only did not get his father's permission, but he also did not tell him of this abrupt change in his plans. Believing the thunderstorm was an actual call from God, he apparently felt no need to *even discuss* this with Hans. Martin

4. Martin Luther, "Letter to Hans Luther" (November 21, 1521), *LW* 48:331.

himself admits in the letter that the father's "indignation against me for a time was implacable."[5]

From the vantage point of seventeen years later, Luther now recognizes that his decision was against the fourth commandment (Honor your father and mother), and moreover, clouded by his own sense of self-righteousness. And while the father's wrath moderated somewhat, as evidenced by his attendance at his son's first mass in 1507, Hans was still upset because, at the reception following this event, he reminded the son that "parents are to be obeyed." Hardly the words of acceptance that Luther was surely longing for! Those words haunted Luther for a long time: "I have hardly ever in my whole life heard any man say anything that struck me so forcibly and stuck to me so long."[6] Quite a statement from someone who was under constant attack for the past four years.

But now, in 1521, everything had changed. God had acted and given Luther a genuine vocation: preacher and teacher of the Word. The Lord's ways are mysterious. Luther says his time in the monastery had actually served a higher purpose for it allowed him time to study the Bible, be trained in theology, and that "the sanctity (!) of the monasteries should become known to me by my own actual experience." Though his monastic vow was not worth a "fig," it allowed him to come under the authority of Christ (his bishop, abbot, lord, and father) and put him in true service of God's Word.[7]

As for his father, this change in calling seems to have improved their relationship. Both Hans and Margaret are present at his surprising wedding in 1525. And we also have

5. Ibid., 331–32.
6. Ibid.
7. Ibid., 333.

from Luther's hand his tender letter to his father in 1530, when Hans is on his deathbed. The son was prevented from coming to his father's side because he was under the ban of the empire and the territory between them was contested. The fourth commandment, originally the source of friction between them, is now something Luther is happy to honor. The note itself brims with gratitude and concern for Hans: "In the meantime I pray from the bottom of my heart that our Father, who has made you my father, will strengthen you according to his immeasurable kindness and enlighten and protect you with his Spirit. . . ." He recognizes that his own vocation has not been easy for Hans.[8] Indeed, Catholic opponents have suggested publicly that Luther's true father was the devil who had intercourse with his mother.[9] And finally, if this illness should lead to death, Luther assures Hans of Christ's abiding presence "so that . . . we may see each other, either here or in the next life."[10]

Hans Luther died about three months after the letter was written. The son was overcome with grief. He wrote the following to his longtime colleague, Philip Melanchthon:

> John Reineck wrote me today that my beloved father, the senior Hans Luther, departed this life at one o'clock on Exaudi Sunday. This death has cast me into deep mourning, not only because of the ties of nature but also because it was through his sweet love to me that my Creator endowed me with all that I am have. Although it is consoling to me, as he writes, my father fell asleep softly and strong in his faith in Christ, yet his kindness and the memory of his pleasant conversation have caused so deep a wound in my heart that I have scarcely ever held death in such low esteem.[11]

8. Martin Luther, *Letters of Spiritual Counsel*, trans. and ed. by Theodore G. Tappert (Philadelphia: Westminster, 1960), 31.
9. Oberman, *Between God and Devil*, 88.
10. Luther, *Letters of Spiritual Counsel*, 32.
11. Ibid., 30.

A remarkable and fitting testimony to the miner who, once again, was returned to the earth.

Luther the Spouse

It is hard to know exactly when Luther's days as a monk came to an end. Even after his excommunication from the church in 1521, he continued his work in Wittenberg, dressed in the cowl of a friar and living in an abandoned monastery. At one point in this period, he even says, "I am still a monk and yet not a monk. I am a new creature, not of the pope, but of Christ."[12] He is quite skeptical of the value of the monastic life by this time; he believes the gift of celibacy is only given to a few and generally feels that most cloisters are infected with works-righteousness. But there is one date where it becomes crystal clear that Luther has left his old life behind: June 13, 1525. This is the day of his marriage to a former nun, Katherine von Bora.

12. Ibid., 262.

Katherine von Bora. Courtesy of Wikimedia Commons.

Long before his own marriage took place, Luther wrote regularly about marriage as a high calling. This ran against the grain of the culture, which tended to place marriage on a lower level than the lives led by monks, nuns, and priests. However, Luther's theological revolution, centered in the idea that we are justified by grace through faith, meant that no one was closer to God by virtue of the kind of life they lived. Vows of celibacy and poverty were admirable—but only if they resulted in the service of neighbor. If used to seek merit with God, they were not only useless; they were dangerous to the soul because they obscured the true meaning of Christ's death on the cross.

The task facing Luther and his rehabilitation of marriage comes into stark relief when compared with the trend of his time to degrade it. He reports his own impressions of marriage in his childhood:

> When I was a boy, the wicked and impure practice of celibacy had made marriage so disreputable that I believed I could not even think about the life of married people without sinning. Everybody was fully persuaded that anyone who intended to lead a holy life acceptable to God could not get married but had to live as a celibate and take a vow of celibacy.[13]

Luther's contemporary, the writer Sebastian Franck did not help matters either. Reflecting the spirit of the times, he collected a book of aphorisms (many from writers of antiquity) designed to poke fun at women and marriage. Among the sayings that Franck included: "If you find things going too well, take a wife" and "If you take a wife you get a devil on your back."[14]

---

13. Karant-Nunn and Wiesner-Hanks, *Luther on Women*, 120.
14. Steven Ozment, *When Fathers Ruled: Family Life in Reformation Europe* (Cambridge, MA: Harvard University Press, 1985), 3.

Luther stood firmly in opposition to opinions such as those of Franck. He frankly acknowledges the challenges of marriage:

> Now observe when that clever harlot, our natural reason . . . look(s) at married life, she turns up her nose and says, "Alas, must I rock the baby, wash its diapers, make its bed, smell its stench, stay up nights with it . . . and on top of that care for my wife, provide for her, labor at my trade, take care of this and take care of that, provide for her. . . . What, should I make such a prisoner of myself? . . . It is better to remain free and lead a peaceful, carefree life. . . ."[15]

But the difficulties of marriage must be kept in perspective. However severe the burdens, they are no match for the Christian faith. It has a different lens by which it sees the world:

> (Christian faith) . . . opens its eyes, looks upon all these insignificant, distasteful, and despised duties in the Spirit, and is aware that they are all adorned with divine approval as with the costliest gold and jewels. It says, "O God, because I am certain that thou hast created me as a man and hast from my body begotten this child, I also know for a certainty that it meets with they perfect pleasure. I confess to thee that I am not worthy to rock the little babe or wash its diapers, . . . O how gladly will I do so, though the duties should be even more insignificant and despised. Neither frost nor heat, neither drudgery nor labor, will distress or dissuade me for I am certain it is pleasing in thy sight. . . ."[16]

Indeed, Luther notes that marriage and its goodness have a basis in creation itself. Adam and Eve were the first married couple. Adam's expression of joy in Genesis 2:23, "This at last is bone of my bones and flesh of my flesh" is genuine and reflects God's own delight in marriage.

However, Luther not only thought and wrote about

---

15. Karant-Nunn and Wiesner-Hanks, *Luther on Women*, 107.
16. Ibid.

marriage, he also had an actual calling as a spouse. He was married to Katherine for over twenty years—about the same amount of time he had spent as a monk. He ended up voting strongly in favor of the domestic realm as a better place to exercise one's Christian faith.

There has been an excess of sentimental bosh written about Luther's marriage. Some of it is horribly sexist and dominated by pictures of a deferential Katherine, who exists merely to wait upon Luther and care for their six children (they also adopted four orphans). It might be appropriate to pause at this point and clear out some of the underbrush on this topic.

In many ways, Luther viewed women like most of his sixteenth century contemporaries. As Wiesner-Hanks and Karant-Nunn point out, Luther did little to modify the image of Eve as the one responsible for the fall of humanity. In general, women were less rational than men (a bad thing) and more prone to emotion (also a bad thing). And he makes clear that a woman's place is in the home. So, in the abstract, a case can be made for Luther being more or less representative of his age when it came to the abilities and roles of women.

But caution is needed here as well. Luther's theories about the nature and calling of women may not be enlightened by our standards. However, his actual relationship with Katherine von Bora is remarkable for its mutual love, respect, and admiration. For example, to label Katherine as a "housewife" hardly does justice to her role.[17] When the prince of Saxony gave them the now-empty Augustinian monastery in Wittenberg for their home, Katherine inherited a job that included managing and overseeing a forty-room building. It was often full of residents that included her ten children,

17. Martin Treu, "Katherine von Bora: The Woman at Luther's Side," *Lutheran Quarterly*, ns 13, no. 2 (Summer 1999), 165–69.

students attending the university, guests of Wittenberg faculty, and religious refugees fleeing persecution. Moreover, she was in charge of the farm linked with the home as well as an orchard and a brewery. And on top of all this, she was married to the volcanic Luther, who was prone to bouts of depression, prodigal with the family money, and under the ban of the Empire (which meant that many powerful people wished her husband dead).

Luther's comments about Katherine express great appreciation and respect. While he admitted that the emotional bond between the two was not deep at first, after five years of marriage, he was fond of referring to his favorite biblical book, Galatians, as his "Katherine von Bora." When Luther slid into deep spiritual shadows, it was often Katherine who ministered to him. In one well-known episode, she appeared before him dressed in black from head to toe. When Luther inquired who had died, Katherine replied, "God must be dead from the way you are acting."[18] Such was his esteem that he once exclaimed that he wouldn't trade her for France or Venice. Half in jest, he also worried that she was a threat to his spiritual life: "I give more credit to Katherine than to Christ, who has done so much more for me."[19]

But Luther was also realistic about the challenges of marriage. Hints of this appear in his Table Talk (a record of Luther's remarks made in the company of friends and often at dinner). As he reflects on Adam and Eve, he also is making reference to his own experience: "Good God, what a lot of trouble there is in marriage. Adam has made a mess of our nature. Think of all the squabbles Adam and Eve must have had

18. Rudolf K. Markwald and Marilynn Morris Markwald, *Katharina von Bora: A Reformation Life* (St. Louis: Concordia, 2002), 140.
19. See Bainton, *Here I Stand*, 228.

in the course of their nine hundred years. Eve would say, 'You ate the apple,' and Adam would retort, 'You gave it to me.'"[20]

In conclusion, two items serve to underline Luther's love and respect for Katherine—one legal, and the other, an exclamation typical of the reformer. Few things reveal a person's priorities like the making of a will. The question looming behind the legal work is this: who can be trusted to take care of that which is most valued in life? Luther, in clear violation of the law of his day, wanted to appoint Katherine, a *woman*, as his sole heir. The legal code stipulated that women could not inherit; property was given to the children, or, if that wasn't possible, to the relatives on the man's side. But Luther, highlighting his esteem of Katherine, as well as her financial acumen, attempted to circumvent the typical way of doing things. In the end, he wasn't successful, but this should not obscure the sentiment.[21]

Perhaps no passage better combines Luther's theology, his views on marriage, and the genuine love and affection he felt for Katherine than the following quote from a wedding sermon he preached in 1531, which would have been six years after his own wedding:

> God's Word is actually inscribed on one's spouse. When a man looks at his wife as if she were the only woman on earth, and when a woman looks at her husband as if he were the only man on earth; yes, if no king or queen, not even the sun itself sparkles any more brightly and lights up your eyes more than your own husband or wife, then right there you are face to face with God speaking. God promised to you your wife or husband, actually gives your spouse to you saying: "The man shall be yours; the woman shall be yours. I am pleased beyond measure! Creatures earthly and heavenly are jumping for joy." For there is no jewelry more precious than God's Word; through it you come to regard

---

20. As quoted in Bainton, *Here I Stand*, 235.
21. Treu, "Katherine von Bora," 170–71.

your spouse as a gift of God and, as long as you do that, you will have no regrets.[22]

It is doubtful such words could have come from one who was not personally acquainted with the deep love and joy of married life.

Martin Luther once said that marriage is a better school for character than any monastery. This was hardly a theoretical statement. Luther spent about the same amount of time in his callings as a monk and a spouse. And he ended up pointing to the domestic realm as a better place to exercise one's Christian faith. Moreover, Luther was not just a spouse. He also became a parent. He was the father of six natural children and perhaps as many as four orphans.

Luther the Parent

We do not have a lot of information about Luther as a father. The external facts are fairly clear. He and Katherine had six children of their own over their twenty-one years of marriage. In addition, they adopted the four children of his sister when she died in 1529. They also raised several other nieces and nephews.[23] When you do the addition, you come up with a least thirteen or fourteen children that were part of the household at various times.

Chaos must have been close at hand in the midst of so many voices clamoring for attention. Katherine and her servants bore the brunt of the responsibility, of course. Further, as his reputation continued to grow, the demands on Luther's time hardly lessened. He continued to write, preach, and

---

22. From a sermon of Luther's as translated by Scott Hendrix in "Luther on Marriage," *Harvesting Martin Luther's Reflections on Theology, Ethics, and the Church* (Grand Rapids: Eerdmans, 2004), 184.
23. Brecht III, 238.

travel—activities that undoubtedly took him away from time with his family. Nevertheless, we do have a few documents that illustrate his calling as parent.

The first example comes actually from a time before Luther was married. Three years before his wedding to Katherine, he wrote a defense of marriage in opposition to the church's view that celibacy was a higher calling. The actual quote is lengthy, but worth reading because it is vintage Luther on vocation:

> Now observe that when that clever harlot, our natural reason (which the pagans followed in trying to be most clever), takes a look at married life, she turns up her nose and says, "Alas, must I rock the baby, wash its diapers, make its bed, smell its stench, stay up nights with it, take care of it when it cries, heal its rashes and sores, and on top of that care for my wife, provide for her, labor at my trade, take care of this and take care of that, do this and do that, endure this and endure that, and whatever else of bitterness and drudgery married life involves? What, should I make such a prisoner of myself? . . .
>
> What then does Christian faith say to this? It opens its eyes, looks upon all these insignificant, distasteful, and despised duties in the Spirit, and is aware that they are all adorned with divine approval as with the costliest gold and jewels. It says, "0 God, because I am certain that thou hast created me as a man and hast from my body begotten this child, I also know for a certainty that it meets with thy perfect pleasure. I confess to thee that I am not worthy to rock the little babe or wash its diapers . . .
>
> Now you tell me, when a father goes ahead and washes diapers or performs some other mean task for his child, and someone ridicules him as an effeminate fool, though that father is acting in the spirit just described and in Christian faith, my dear fellow you tell me, which of the two is most keenly ridiculing the other? God, with all his angels and creatures, is smiling, not because that father is washing diapers, but because he is doing so in Christian faith. Those who sneer at him and see only the task but not the faith are ridiculing God with all his creatures, as the biggest fool on earth. Indeed, they are only ridiculing themselves; with all their cleverness they are nothing but devil's fools.[24]

One cannot help but wonder if Luther might have still lauded the task of changing diapers, say ten years later, when such a job would have been a regular feature of his life! But his overall point remains. The mundane duties of parenthood are not to be despised. In fact, there is no more honorable calling than to be deeply involved in the smells, dirt, laughter, and tears of domestic life.

When it comes to the actual vocation of fatherhood, we have two letters from Luther to his oldest son, Hans. The first is written when the boy is four years old. Luther tells Hans of a charming garden with "nice apples, pears, cherries and plums." All the children in this place wear golden coats and have little horses with silver saddles. Moreover, the place is alive with sounds of drums and lutes. The children in the garden are dancing and even practicing shooting with small crossbows. Luther tells his son that all this awaits him if he is diligent in study and prayer.[25]

A second letter comes from a time when Hans is probably in his early teens. The tone in this note is not as warm. While Luther praises his son for his work in his studies, one also gets the impression that Hans has given evidence of being overly interested in things not connected with his schooling. He admonishes him to keep his focus on God and his blessings and to "not let himself be diverted by bad examples." Luther reminds Hans that God has not only provided blessings, but will also punish those who stray from his path. One sentence in particular stands out. Luther tells his son to "fear God and listen to your parents, who surely want only the best for you, and flee from shameful and dishonorable company." We lack

---

24. Martin Luther, "The Estate of Marriage," (1522), *LW* 45:39–41.
25. *TR* 5:377–78.

a wider context, but the picture appears to be one of a father who is calling out a son who has fallen out of line.[26]

Luther also knew great sorrow as a parent. Martin and Katherine's second child, Elizabeth, died when she was nine months old. But most difficult of all was the passing of fourteen-year-old Magdalene in 1542. She died in her father's arms after a brief illness. In her last moments, Luther asked her if she would go happily to her father in heaven. Replied the sick Magdalene: "Yes, dear Father as God wills." Katherine was reportedly so overcome with grief that she stayed on the other side of the room. Luther tried to comfort her with the following words: "Remember where she is going. It will be well with her. The flesh dies but the spirit lives. Children do not argue . . . (to them) everything is plain. They die without anxiety, without complaint, without fear of death, without great physical pain, just as if they were falling asleep."[27]

The death of a child cuts deep. It violates the natural order of things and frequently sends the parents into a downward spiral of grief. Doubtless, Luther found great comfort in the promise: "Whether we live or whether we die we are the Lord's" (Romans 14:8).[28] But he also reportedly said of Magdalene's death: "How strange it is to know that she is at peace and all is well and yet to be so sorrowful."[29] Luther knew that sorrow did not have the final word. But the loss of a fourteen-year-old child, even in a culture well-acquainted with the death of children, had to be a severe blow. No wonder that the aging Luther (he was four years from his own death), as a result of losing his daughter, reported a longing for his own death and a deliverance from the evils of this life.[30]

26. TR 8:18–20.
27. Tappert, *Letters of Spiritual Counsel*, 50–51.
28. Ibid., 51.
29. As quoted in Bainton, *Here I Stand*, 237.

What Does This Mean?

When I think of family life, I immediately think of the word "ordinary." Now, to be sure, not everything about families is simple or ordinary. In fact, many memories stand out as extraordinary: the birth of a child, a wedding day, the death of a parent. But, for the most part, the time spent in family is more or less pretty mundane. Think of the hours spent helping children with homework or talking with spouses about finances or tending to the needs of an elderly parent or listening to the concerns of a brother or sister. For most of us, at the end of our days, time spent in the company of family will dwarf commitments elsewhere. And this points to a huge problem in the contemporary understanding of vocation.

Far too much of our discussion on vocation focuses on the extraordinary. A few years back, my college sponsored a series of lectures on vocation. I remember one speaker, sweaty-browed, who challenged students to seize the ONE life they were given and to make it EXTRAORDINARY. He repeated one question throughout his talk: What one wild and outrageous thing are you going to do with your life? On one level, this type of rhetoric works. We want our young people to be idealistic and dream big dreams. But the underlying presupposition is that this is what vocation is really about: doing something exceptional with your life.

However, that ignores the basic realities of living, and in particular, the humdrum of family life. God must love the ordinary because so much of our time is spent in our homes, just tending to basic *stuff*. The writer Jerry Sittser puts it this way: Anyone who lives to the age of eighty will live about 29,200 days or 700,800 hours. Of those hours, a person will

30. Brecht III, 238.

spend roughly 2,000 hours brushing her teeth, 204,000 hours sleeping, 43,800 hours eating, and 58,400 hours doing chores.[31] And, of course, much of this time will be spent with other people—namely spouses, children, siblings, and parents.

Given the importance of family life, and especially, the fact that the domestic sphere is where we spend many of our waking (and sleeping) hours, what does it mean to have a sense of calling in this realm?

As a college professor and Lutheran pastor, it is one of my great privileges and joys to attend the weddings of some of my students. On occasion, I am asked to give the homily at the ceremony. Sometimes, I bring three "props"—a rock, a wine glass, and a towel—to use as illustrations in the message. The first object, a rock, is taken from an encounter in an old country cemetery in rural Norway. As I wandered around, I noticed the saying "Tak for alt" inscribed on many of the markers. Often, small stones had been placed on the gravesites as well. A caretaker was nearby and I asked him what this meant. The saying "Tak for alt" means "thanks for everything" in Norwegian. Family members and friends who had visited the grave placed the small stones. In what, for me, was a very moving conversation, the caretaker said the saying and the stones represented a sense of gratitude for the life that was lived. I recall his eyes sparkling as he commented: "If we forget to be thankful then we have missed the whole thing."

The second item is a wine glass. I took this idea from Jewish wedding ceremonies, which often conclude with the breaking of a glass and the shout of "Mazel Tov." The breaking of the goblet symbolizes the fragility of life. It is a way to remind the couple that in the midst of the joy of a wedding day, there will also be sadness and difficulty on the journey ahead.

---

31. Jerry Sittser, *The Will of God as a Way of Life* (Grand Rapids: Zondervan, 2004), 83–93.

The third item is a towel. In the Gospel of John, we are told that shortly before his death, Jesus gathered his disciples together and washed their feet. Remember in the world of the New Testament that people wore sandals and feet were dirty. The role of the servant, most dramatically displayed by Jesus' death on the cross, is foreshadowed in the very mundane act of washing feet.

A rock, a glass and a towel—what does all of this have to do with vocation? In marriage and family life, we find ourselves immersed in the nitty-gritty. We bump into one another frequently, and often, our elbows are sharp. Children compete for time and attention. Illness often intrudes in cruel ways that tests patience and endurance. Harsh words are spoken in the heat of the moment, creating grudges and distance. In some ways, our families and marriages are testing grounds like no other. In many cases, spouses and family members start "keeping score" and become sunk in themselves, their worlds framed by "me" and "mine" while the sense of the greater good is lost.

A called life approaches the domestic realm in a different way. Our baptism into Christ means that we start with a word of gratitude. We are reminded that our identity rests in God's love—a love that is greater than anything we can possibly conceive. Moreover, that baptismal grace is part of veritable shower of other blessings. "What do you have that you did not receive?' asks the apostle Paul in I Corinthians 4:7. Indeed, generations before us with their incredible sacrifices make our present life possible. Friends have supported us through times bad and good. Teachers and co-workers have been patient with our questions and shortcomings. And that does not even take into account the material blessings that pour forth from God's hand through the efforts of others. Vocation is inseparable from a sense of gratitude—a "Tak for alt" view of life.

All of this is not to diminish the obstacles that will come our way. The breaking of the glass reminds us that all will not be well. Loving our neighbors who are nearest to us is the most difficult task we will face. As we have seen, Luther stressed that we not only bear Christ is our callings, but also, that Christ comes to us in the faces of those closest to us. We would prefer to arrange our service to suit our own needs and timetables. But marriage and family life upends that way of thinking. In the neighbor—read spouse, parent, child, brother, sister—Christ comes to us, interrupting our schedules and breaking our preferred patterns of proceeding. Christ comes as the teenager full of anxiety and rebellion. Christ comes as the spouse overwhelmed by work. Christ comes as brother or sister who has just lost a job or is going through a difficult divorce. Christ comes as the elderly parent who is lonely and grieving. In the realm of vocation, and this is most evident in the domestic sphere, Christ simply refuses to leave us alone.[32]

As a result, we need to take up our towels for we will always have plenty to do. Shaped by the power of baptism, we seek to serve humbly and listen patiently to the needs and concerns of those nearest to us. This is what it means to die daily in our baptism. But there is a rising as well. A surprising fruit of our calling in the domestic realm could perhaps be a sense of joy. If sought on its own, joy (like happiness) is almost always elusive. However, when we serve the "least of these" (see Matt. 25:31-46) in our callings, we just might find ourselves

---

32. By identifying Christ with the neighbor, one has to be careful as some discernment is in order. When the neighbor is destructive (an abusive spouse, for example), the call to love might first mean removing oneself from a dangerous situation. Love does not sanction abuse for the sake of stability.

possessed of a blessedness that far surpasses anything we might have expected.

Questions for Discussion

Using the images of a rock, a glass, and a towel (mentioned above), reflect on your sense of calling in your family and your marriage (if that applies).

1. What are you thankful for?
2. Where are the struggles and biggest areas of difficulty?
3. Can you lift up some examples of love and service in your family (or in your family's history) that have been particularly meaningful?
4. How do you imagine the vocation of love and service playing out in your life?

6

Called to Be a Citizen

Therefore should you see that there is a lack of hangmen, beadles, judges, lords or princes and you should find that you are qualified, you should offer your services and apply for the position so that necessary government may be no means be despised and become inefficient or perish. For the world cannot and dare not dispense with it.[1]

Our study of Luther and the called life now extends outward from the personal and domestic realm to that of citizen. To speak of Luther and citizenship verges on anachronism. For most people, "citizen" connotes participation in a political process. It harkens back to the classical period, when a small number of citizens out of the total population took responsibility for managing the affairs of the *polis* or city state. The Germany of Luther's day was far removed from the concept of democracy as it is now understood. Luther's own

---

1. Martin Luther, "Secular Authority: To What Extent it Should Be Obeyed" (1523), *LW* 45:95.

rulers in Saxony were hereditary leaders. Power was handed down within family dynasties and the ruled had little choice over who would exercise dominion over them. Luther could not have conceived of citizen participation in a democratic process where people vote leaders in and out of office.

But Luther was heavily involved in politics. He could hardly have avoided it, given the way church and state overlapped in sixteenth-century Europe—something he deeply lamented. Our use of "citizen" is retained, however, because this is a study of how Luther's own vocation might inform our understanding of our own callings. We use the term "citizen," however advisedly, because we are not dealing primarily with Luther's theory of government. Many studies have adequately covered that topic. Rather, we want to review some cases that show how Luther actually acted politically, and then, mine those insights in order to reflect on our calling as citizens today. As already mentioned, a good theology of vocation fights abstraction. We are using Luther so that we ourselves might think more concretely about how to live a called life in the public realm.

"Politics" Is Not a Dirty Word

Many studies of Luther and the political realm begin with situations laden with great drama—his appearance before the Emperor, princes, and bishops at Diet of Worms in 1521 or his involvement in the Peasants' Rebellion of 1525. But it might be helpful to leave those highly charged episodes for later in the chapter. Instead, let's look at three relatively unknown incidents and see what they might say about Luther and his engagement with matters political.

As already noted, Luther's revolutionary understanding of

vocation meant the closing of many monasteries where the reform movement took hold. As might be imagined, the buildings, property, and foundations belonging to monks were quite valuable. For example, in England, when the royal coffers were in a sad state, King Henry VIII bolstered his financial fortunes by dissolving the monasteries and nunneries and transferring their accumulated wealth to the crown. Similar scenes, on a much smaller scale, took place throughout northern Europe. When King Frederick I of Denmark closed the monasteries in the city of Kiel, he shifted their wealth to the town. But that created new problems because disputes arose about how to dispose of the property. In 1544, the city council in Kiel turned to Luther and asked for his assistance in the matter. Moreover, they hoped his advice would be in "accordance with the Holy Scriptures."[2]

Luther responds in the following way. He thinks it would be wise to give the proceeds of the monasteries to the churches and to the poor of the town. That is the general principle. But he refuses to be more specific and there is also a notable absence of quotations from the Bible. Instead, he counsels the city leaders in the following manner:

> We theologians have nothing to do with determining who is entitled to this FIX property or to whom it shall belong, for we are not commanded to do this, nor are we in a position to know the circumstances. This must be decided by the jurists after inquiring into both sides of the question. . . . For this is a worldly matter and such things have been committed to the jurists. Our theology teaches that secular law is to be observed for the punishment of evildoers and the protection of them that do well. . . . It is not our function as theologians to give a hearing to two parties in a dispute. . . .[3]

2. Luther, *Spiritual Counsel*, 347.
3. Ibid.

We will return to this example in a moment. But first, let's examine two other cases where Luther is asked for advice on a political issue. One concerns a letter of 1525 in response to a ruler in the principality of Brandenburg (north of Wittenberg). Margrave George reports his intention to reform the churches in the area and also properly dispose off the assets of the monasteries that have been closed. In this case, there is no dispute about the funds. Rather, Margrave George is asking for Luther's guidance about what to do with the money. After saying that the former inhabitants of the closed institutions should be properly cared for, Luther continues with recommendations about how to spend the money:

> In the second place, it would be good if in Your Grace's principality Your Grace would establish one or two universities, where not only the Holy Scriptures but also law and all the sciences would be taught. From these schools learned men could be got as preachers, pastors, secretaries, councilors, etc., for the whole principality. . . . If studying is to be encouraged, you must have, not empty cloisters and deserted monasteries and endowed churches, but a city in which many people come together, work together, and incite and stimulate one another. . . . In the third place, it is well that in all towns and villages good primary schools be established.[4]

And finally, let's look at one more situation. This one hits close to home (literally) as it concerns the actions in 1541 of Count Albert of Mansfeld, who ruled the territory where the city of Eisleben was located, the place of Luther's birth and where he would eventually die. Though initially, he was a friend of the Reformation, Albert was also greedy as evidenced by his confiscation of mines and forges in the area—property that was traditionally kept within the control of local families

---

4. Ibid., 325.

for generations. Luther doesn't mince words as he criticizes the Count:

> But it appears to me, especially from rumors and complaints that have reached me, that Your Grace has fallen away from such good beginnings and has become a very different person. . . . Your Grace too must be aware that you have become cold, have given your heart to Mammon, and have the ambition to become very rich. According to complaints your Grace is also sharply and severely oppressive to your subjects and proposed to confiscate their forges and goods and to make what amounts to vassals out of them. God will not suffer this. . . . I pray again that your Grace may be more gentle and gracious with your subjects. Let them remain as before. . . . In short, I am concerned about Your Grace's soul. I cannot permit myself to cease praying for you and being concerned about you, for then I am convinced I would cease being in the Church. . . .[5]

What do these three cases say about Luther's calling in the public realm? First of all, they highlight his belief that Christians are not to shun the world of politics as something "unholy" and beyond their concern. When Luther left the monastery and married, he did not confine his concerns to the home and the church. Rather, he knew that Christian love of neighbor includes not just those close at hand, but also those at a distance. And this inevitably meant getting involved in the public realm. Luther believed Count Albert of Mansfeld was hurting his subjects with his greed, so he called him to account. Luther also knew the value of education for making communities stronger, so he counseled Margrave George to provide for universities and schools in Brandenburg.

Second, Luther is cautious about using the Bible to prescribe how people should live. God's good gift of human reason can do a fine job in ordering human affairs. One is mindful of the crack

5. Ibid., 338.

allegedly attributed to him that "he would rather be ruled by a smart Turk than a dumb Christian." When the city leaders of Kiel asked for guidance about a specific dispute, he resisted the temptation to quote Scripture as a way to solve their problem. Basically, he tells them to let the lawyers handle the matter.

Third, Luther understands his calling in the public realm means there will be occasions when bold speech is needed. He does not shrink from the prophetic task of naming egregious public sins—especially when they hurt the unprotected and poor. The untrammeled greed of Count Albert is challenged forthrightly. Luther calls him "cold" and really says that he is guilty of idolatry and blasphemy because he has traded worship of the true God for the false god of wealth. Some might say that Luther speaks from a position of power and privilege in this episode. After all, he is now the hallowed leader of the Reformation, and therefore, immune from any consequences. But this objection does not quite ring true. Recall that some twenty years earlier, at the Diet of Worms, Luther spoke just as boldly to the powers and principalities that had gathered to hear him. At the time, he was a mere monk and a teacher at university that did not have much of a reputation. He rightly expected to die for his cause, but his conscience molded by his faith led him to speak courageously.

Luther and the Peasants

We are now better prepared to discuss the most famous episode where Luther exercised his calling in the political realm: the Peasants' Rebellion of 1525. Some background is necessary in order to understand the situation.

The life of a peasant in Luther's age was, to say the least, not easy. The great English thinker, Thomas Hobbes, would in the next century memorably characterize the state of nature as "nasty, brutish and short." Average life expectancy was probably close to forty years old. Infant mortality rates were alarmingly high. The vast majority of people could not read or write. Moreover, nature's cruelty was on full display in the form of famine, drought, flood, and disease. All of this would be difficult enough, but in Luther's day the nobility (those who owned the land) often made the situation even worse. They leveled onerous death taxes on the peasants, taking valuable property when someone in the family died. Moreover, the combination of rising inflation, over-population, and the widespread appropriation of common land (which peasants used for grazing their cattle) by landlords led to almost intolerable conditions. The peasants were often stretched to the breaking point, as evidenced by some 150 revolts of various sizes in Germany in the early part of the sixteenth century.[6]

A major rebellion broke out in 1524–25 and Luther soon found himself in the midst of the conflict as it spread into central Germany. Luther found fault with both sides of the conflict. The rulers should not be surprised by the violence of their subjects. After all, they had treated the common people with contempt and little concern for justice:

> We have no one on earth to blame for his disastrous rebellion except you princes and Lords and especially you blind bishops and mad priests . . . as temporal rulers you do nothing but cheat and rob the people so that you may lead lives of luxury.[7]

But he was also impatient with the peasants. Part of their demands included a political program based on "Christian"

6. Kolb, *Confessor of the Faith*, 187.
7. Martin Luther, "Admonition to Peace, A Reply to the Twelve Articles of the Peasants in Swabia" (1525), LW 46:19.

principles. For example, they argued that Christian freedom legitimated the freedom from political serfdom.

Peasants working. Courtesy of Wikimedia Commons.

They also suggested that prohibitions on hunting and fishing were against Scripture because in Genesis 1, God had given humanity authority over animals. The appeal to the Bible rankled Luther because it suggested that the revolt was a Christian one. He was probably also alarmed because he was among the authorities appealed to by the peasants to justify their cause. But Luther was wary of identifying any political program as "Christian." While he certainly supported general principles such as caring for the poor and vulnerable (and he recognized the complaints of the common people were just), he saw a potential for great mischief when political leaders claim God's blessing and support for their specific platforms—especially ones where bloodshed and vengeance were part of the equation, as was the case with the peasants.

When the revolt continued unabated, Luther became alarmed that the whole land would be engulfed in chaos. On a preaching tour in an area close to Wittenberg, he witnessed first-hand the passionate mobs of peasants and their unwillingness to listen to reason. Indiscriminate attacks of violence led him to take up his pen once again. This time, he forcefully urged the princes to restore order:

> Rebellion is not just simple murder; it is like a great fire which attacks and devastates an entire land. Thus rebellion brings with it a land filled with murder and bloodshed; it makes orphans and widows and turns everything upside down . . . therefore let everyone who can, smite, slay and stab . . . remembering that nothing can be more poisonous, hurtful or devilish than a rebel. It is just as when one must kill a mad dog; it you do not strike him he will strike you and the whole land with you.[8]

This infamous section of the treatise does not reveal Luther at his best. The language was intemperate and incendiary and causes the reader to wince. For good reason, it continues to haunt his legacy up to the present day.

But it is also easy to project our own standards back to the time of Luther. While Luther was sympathetic to the plight of the peasants, he could never have imagined redressing their grievances by means of a social welfare system—like we have today. He knew from his own family that the lot of common people was hard, but he was suspicious of any egalitarian scheme to share wealth equally, particularly one based on "biblical principles." As stated earlier, he lived two centuries before the democratic revolutions that enabled the masses to gain a measure of wealth and political power.

But it should also be pointed out that Luther is consistent with the political principles described earlier in the chapter. The Peasants' Rebellion shows the reformer deeply engaged in the political world—even if we might wish for him to be

8. Martin Luther, "Against the Robbing and Murderous Hordes of Peasants," *LW* 46:50.

wiser in his guidance to the princes. Moreover, he resists the temptation to rule the world by "Christian" principles and also speaks boldly to those in power. Having looked at Luther exercising his calling in a variety of contexts, perhaps it is now time to step back and review the theological framework that he believes ought to govern the Christian in the messy world of politics.

God's World, Two Kingdoms

A good place to begin when talking about Luther's views on politics is to stress that the whole world belongs to God and that God continues to rule over it. The division into a "sacred" and "secular" realm, where the latter implies an absence of God, was completely foreign to the reformer. God remains the one who creates and preserves the entire world. This is a bedrock principle for Luther.

Luther does recognize, however, that God operates in two different ways. This is necessary because humanity has an inordinate degree of self-concern. If God attempted to rule the unruly by a standard that stressed mercy and forgiveness, then chaos and disorder would result. Luther's own picturesque language says it best:

> It would be like a shepherd who put together in one fold wolves, lions, eagles and sheep and let them mingle freely with one another saying: "Help yourselves to food and be good and peaceful to one another. The sheep would doubtless keep the peace but they would not last long. Neither would one beast survive another."[9]

---

9. Martin Luther, "Temporal Authority: To What Extent It Should Be Obeyed" (1523), *LW* 45:92.

In other words, to attempt to order the world by the yardstick of the gospel would yield only violence and theft.

At the same time, Luther recognizes that it is not possible to produce Christian righteousness by means of the law (which is needed to keep order). His false calling as a monk made him realize that any attempt to justify ourselves on the basis of the law either leads to despair (we always fall short) or arrogance (we think we deserve God's love and mercy). So, there is another sphere (kingdom), which is normed by the liberating Word that God loves the "ungodly" (Rom. 5:6). The cross of Christ extends over this entire realm, forgiving sinners and welcoming outcasts.

So, as some have suggested, God is ambidextrous, ruling over his world with two hands—the law (left) and the gospel (right). Again, Luther supplies a fine explanation:

> For this reason one must carefully distinguish between these two governments. Both must be permitted to remain; the one to produce righteousness, the other to bring about external peace and prevent evil deeds. Neither one is sufficient in the world without the other. No one can become righteous in the sight of God by means of the temporal government, without Christ's spiritual government. . . . On the other hand, where the spiritual government alone prevails over land and people, there wickedness is given free reign and the door is open for all manner of rascality, for the world as a whole cannot receive or comprehend it.[10]

Note that, for Luther, the temporal realm remains in God's control. God exercises his rule in that realm in all sorts of ways. Some are negative—the image of the soldier going to war to defend his nation or the police officer stopping the car weaving in traffic because she suspects drunk driving—describe roles in the world that are needed to keep chaos at bay. But there

10. Ibid.

are also positive pictures—the politician proposing laws or the teacher instructing students on citizenship—both are tasks needed to keep the world running well. And behind all these callings (Luther refers to them as God's "masks") stands God, who uses human beings to preserve and extend peace and order.

Historically, this has proven to be a slippery teaching. It has sometimes been interpreted as though the temporal kingdom stands on its own (is purely secular), but this would be a fundamental denial of Luther's profound understanding of vocation. Others have interpreted the worldly realm as ruled by God, but in a very static way. In this view, the politician, teacher, or police officer is appointed by God, and therefore, beyond question. In other words, divine authority is lodged in worldly callings, and thus, they must not be criticized. This is also a perversion of Luther's views. For him, ultimate authority always resided with God and not with the person holding a particular position. Just because God can work through the politician, it does not mean the politician becomes God. Again, to perhaps belabor the point, all callings are from God, who remains the ultimate standard behind all attempts to order the world in justice and peace.

What Does This Mean?

Faith and politics. There are few topics that create more confusion or tension. It is said that they should be avoided in polite conversation because, presumably, of their incendiary qualities. Both touch on matters near and dear to the human heart. This also means they are subject to much passion and disagreement. Better to avoid them altogether or, at the very least, keep our opinions to ourselves. But our calling as citizens allows us no such luxury. As Luther makes clear, we have a vocation to be involved in the world and this includes politics. It might be useful to begin by clearing away some of the cultural underbrush on this topic. And then, we can proceed to construct a framework for thinking about how Christians might exercise love of neighbor in the political realm.

First of all, in an American context, there is a significant difference between the proper relationship of faith and politics and the separation of church and state. The Bill of Rights in the United States Constitution says that no religion will become the official faith of the country. With regard to religion, Americans are free to practice the faith of their own choosing. But this "wall of separation" between church and state does not mean that faith has no role to play in the public sphere.

Our vocation as citizens necessarily includes service in the community. And that includes politics. It is yet another way we serve our neighbor. This can take various forms. It might mean helping with a voluntary organization, such as scouts or a school organization. It may involve serving in elective office or attending a caucus or participating in an advocacy group. Our overall goal is to make sure justice is done and the health of the community (city, state, nation) is improved. How would it be possible to leave faith out of the picture? When I vote for a particular politician or referendum, I am making judgments about how I would like the world to be. My faith provides (or it should) me with a vision of society where justice is done and I make my choices accordingly. As we have stressed, this is messy and often it is not straightforward. Faith provides the guiding principles (all people are created good, the neighbor must be loved, etc.) that inform particular choices. But it is difficult to claim that our specific decisions (who gets elected to city council, for example) are a direct reflection of God's will. That would be claiming far too much and suggests we have access to knowledge that is far beyond us. As Isaiah 55:8 reminds us, the ways of the Lord are not necessarily our ways.

As we can see from our survey of Luther's experience with politics, it appears that people typically make two mistakes when it comes to this topic. The first is to retreat from the world and assume that faith is something "private," with no bearing on public life. In this view, Christianity must not be tainted by the world and its compromises. This is the monastic alternative—the world is of the devil and it is best to leave it to its own devices. For folks in this camp, their calling is "higher" and serves the Lord alone—and at a safe distance from the wheeling and dealing of legislative cloakrooms.

It ought to be obvious from our own history that this option has been tried and found wanting. It is built on a false theological foundation that fails to recognize the world as *God's creation*, and therefore, an arena of service. In other words, we are not able to write-off or ignore anything that God has claimed. And that includes God's good, green earth, the assembly halls in state capitals, the gritty street corners of urban America, and the people who populate all of them. Twentieth-century history raises some particularly ominous warnings for those who want to keep faith out of politics. The Lutheran martyr Dietrich Bonhoeffer was horrified by the ability of Christians to look the other way when the vulnerable, the weak, and the Jews were deemed unworthy of life. Most memorably, he said:

> We are not Christ, but if we want to be Christians, we must have some share in Christ's largeheartedness by acting with responsibility and in freedom when the hour of danger comes, and be showing a real compassion that springs, not from fear, but from the liberating and redeeming love of Christ for all who suffer. Mere waiting and looking on is not Christian behavior.

Christians are called to compassion and action, not in the first place by their own sufferings, but by the sufferings of their brothers and sisters, for whose sake Christ suffered.[11]

Dietrich Bonhoeffer.

A second problem comes from the opposite side and happens when Christians seek to baptize their politics. In other words, they confuse their human attempt to achieve justice in the world with the actual will of God. But by what authority do we act in the Lord's name in the political arena? It is true we are called to work for justice in the world. But my view of what that looks like might be very different from the perspective of

11. Dietrich Bonhoeffer, *A Testatment to Freedom. The Essential Writings of Dietrich Bonhoeffer*, ed. by Geffrey B. Kelly and F. Burton Nelson (Harper: New York, 1990), 483–84.

another Christian. For example, I have strong opinions about the United States government's policies toward Israel or how we should attend to the problems of the inner cities. But I have no "Word of the Lord" on this issue. There is no such thing as a "Christian" foreign policy or a "Christian" urban policy. Does that mean we have nothing at all to say?

As hinted earlier, I would argue that we do have principles that cannot be compromised. Some of these "core values" would be that God is good and in charge and that God's creation (including humanity) is good; that we are fallen creatures saved by grace and not our good works; that we are commanded to love our neighbors, take care of creation, seek justice in society and keep a special eye out for the vulnerable, weak, and marginalized. Advocacy of these principles would hardly point to a silent or passive faith. But the mischief begins when we seek to drill down to the particular and make concrete connections between our faith and policy. Does cutting taxes or raising taxes make our society more just? I have opinions backed by what I believe are strong arguments. But I can't claim divine support for my view. Should we spend more on defense? Again, I have my thoughts, but I am not willing to make an absolute (thus sayeth the Lord) type of claim.

So, as Christians, we are called to enter the public realm and work for the vision of a just society.[12] This is contrary to those who would keep faith in a private prayer closet or only within the walls of a church. But our work in the world must be done with humility and the understanding that we could be wrong (against those who wish to baptize their politics). In

---

12. See Ronald W. Duty, "Moral Deliberation in a Public Lutheran Church," *Dialog* 45,4 (Winter 2006) for a nice summary of some contemporary Lutheran theologians' views on how the church relates to the world.

fact, humility makes for healthy politics. When we recognize our positions are somewhat short of the Lord's, we are more likely to listen to what others have to say and actually learn from them. Conversation is stronger. Relationships grow. Who knows, this might even result in justice actually being done.

Let me relate a story from my own experience as a parish pastor as one example of the way faith communities can engage positively in the public realm. My congregation (actually, I was an associate pastor on a staff) was largely white and a mix of middle and working-class folks. It was located in an inner-ring suburb of Minneapolis. My specific calling in the church was to direct its education and community outreach programs. Our entire staff and lay leadership believed deeply that God has called us to be engaged in the world of politics without falling into the temptation of claiming that our points of view are God's own perspective.

Our challenge was how to translate that conviction into the everyday life of the community. We did three things. First, in our preaching, teaching, and newsletters (this was before websites!), we made a commitment to address public issues we thought Christians ought to think about. We did a sermon series on a range of issues linked with human sexuality—topics such as divorce, homosexuality, sex outside of marriage, and so on. We also did a series on America's place in the world and how Christians had to balance a sense of loyalty to the nation with the recognition that our country could also be wrong. Second, we made a commitment to pray in worship about matters political. Again, we stressed the need not to politicize the prayers, but rather, lift up with regularity the issues most of us would prefer to ignore—the hungry and poor in our midst, our nation's ongoing battle with racism (not forgetting that this is a matter for every American to think about), and so on. And finally, we arranged a series of discussions on what we called "Hot Topics." This last initiative deserves a little extra attention.

There was significant interest in the Hot Topics forum, as forty to fifty people regularly attended. And it was largely successful. I think it worked because we set firm ground rules, rooted in our Christian identity, at our first meeting. We began by stressing that God has called us to this work and that all people are created in God's image and that we were charged with making the world a more just place. We underlined that there was not a "God position" on any of the issues. Our Lutheran convictions provided us the freedom to look at these topics—and disagree about them—without being disrespectful of those who had differing viewpoints. We tackled a wide range of subjects (and remember this was the early 1990s)—the relationship between America and Russia, the Israeli–Palestinian issue, abortion, homosexuality, the social safety net, black-white relations, and so on. I am not saying it always went smoothly. As I recall, our abortion discussion got a bit tense. But overall, it did work and I think those in attendance appreciated that their church could be a place where politics were openly discussed *and* faith convictions were not relegated to the sidelines. Moreover, it made the participants think about how their Christian faith is for the sake of the world—even the messy world of politics—and not an escape from it.

Our present political situation could use the seasoning provided by vocation. Too often, our positions become ultimate and we refuse to listen to the other side. Civil conversation is rare while the loud and rude take center stage. It is critical that we grasp the need to serve our brothers and sisters in the world. God clearly has a stake in the well-being of his creation. In the Bible, the references to the poor and needy and our obligation to serve them far outnumbers any other moral issue. We cannot pretend our vocation as citizens is secondary or less important than our other callings. Perhaps it is best to end this section with the famous verse from the prophet Micah because it beautifully sounds the notes of a passion for justice coupled with humility: "He has told you, O mortal, what is good; and what does the Lord require of you but to do justice, and to love kindness, and to walk humbly with your God" (Micah 6:8)?

Questions for Discussion

1. Discuss Luther's response to the rebellion of the peasants. What do you think of his response to this situation?
2. Can you think of examples of Christians today (on the right and left) who attempt to "baptize" their politics?
3. What do you think of the core values (see pages 111 and 112) that inform our calling in the world of politics? What would you add or subtract from the list?
4. The author proposes something like a "Hot Topics" forum as a way for faith communities to address contemporary issues. What do you think of this idea? Would it work in your community? Why or why not?

7

Called to Christian Community

For attaining such forgiveness of guilt and for calming the heart in the face of its sins, there are various ways and methods. Some think to accomplish this through letters of indulgence. They run to and fro, to Rome or to St. James, buying indulgences here and there. But this is all mistaken and all in vain. Things thereby get much worse.[1]

In the year 1516, Luther is in Wittenberg, where he is called to teach in the university and preach in the city's main church. He is also an Augustinian monk and has risen to a place of leadership as the district vicar of his order. It is in this role that he writes a letter to a fellow monk, George Spenlein, who recently transferred to another monastery in southern Germany. The note begins by discussing some personal matters regarding the disposal of belongings that Spenlein had left behind. But the body of the letter is concerned with the state of Spenlein's soul. Luther wants to know if his fellow monk is

1. Martin Luther, "The Sacrament of Penance" (1519), *LW* 35:10.

tired of trying to achieve righteousness on his own instead of trusting in the mercy of Christ. Apparently, Spenlein believed human effort played a strong role in establishing a saving relationship with God. Luther hopes he has seen the error of his ways and lays out before his fellow brother the new understanding of justification:

> Therefore, my dear brother, learn Christ and him crucified. Learn to pray to him and despairing of yourself, say: "Thou, Lord Jesus, art my righteousness, but I am thy sin. Thou has taken upon thyself what is mine and hast given to me what is thine." . . . Beware of aspiring to such purity that you will not be looked upon as a sinner, or to be one. For Christ dwells only in sinners. . . . Meditate on this love of his and you will see his sweet consolation. For why was it necessary for him to die if we can obtain a good conscience by our works and afflictions?[2]

We begin here in our discussion of Luther's calling in the church because this early letter (one year before he posts the Ninety-five Theses) illustrates a theme that will define the reformer's relationship with both the wider Christian community and his own involvement in the local congregation in Wittenberg. That is, Luther's labors in the church were directed toward pastoral care or what used to be called the "cure of souls." Above all, Luther was concerned about consciences burdened by the deceptive belief that any measure of human effort could make one right with God.

In one sense, Luther's vocation in the church is the story of his life and a comprehensive view of this topic is far beyond the limits of this study. But we can obtain a glimpse of Luther's calling in the church by focusing on his activity at two very different levels. First, we will spotlight the dramatic Luther who unwittingly finds himself on the world historical stage.

---

2. Luther, *Spiritual Counsel*, 110.

This is the better-known side of the reformer—the German Hercules who takes an axe and hews down the tree of corruption. The context here is the controversy over the sale of indulgences.

Luther as German Hercules. Courtesy of Wikimedia Commons.

And then, we will shift our perspective to the small city of Wittenberg and Luther's calling as a preacher in the city's main church. Here, we will look at his vocation as a preacher who was called to challenge his congregation when they became lazy or self-satisfied as well as the pastor who sought to comfort his people with the message of the gospel. We will conclude with a surprising glance at some of the frustrations he faced when he realizes that his listeners are not taking him or God's Word seriously.

The Wild Boar in the Vineyard

As the truth of justification by grace through faith impressed itself more and more on Luther, it became inevitable that he would collide with some questionable practices of the church of his day. This was certainly the case with the sale of indulgences. Some background is necessary in order to appreciate why the Ninety-five Theses have traditionally been used to mark the starting point of the Reformation.

We have already noted in the second chapter the importance of the sacrament of penance in the life of the medieval church. Baptism was significant for it washed away the stain of original sin. But it soon faded into the mists of infancy. For sins committed after baptism, penance was necessary for reconciliation with God. The sacrament essentially involved the following process: sorrow for sin and confession to a priest, absolution, and a work of satisfaction. At the core of the sacrament is the idea that the sinner had created a debt to God and to society. When a priest absolved a penitent, the debt to God was forgiven. But the sacrament was still not complete. The work of satisfaction, as the last segment in this sequence, was designed ideally to deepen the soul's relationship with God (for example, five recitations of the Lord's Prayer), and also, to balance the temporal debt incurred by the confessed infraction. It is at this point that the sale of indulgences becomes part of the narrative.

In the medieval period, the church began teaching that one could purchase an indulgence (literally a "kindness") to substitute for the work of satisfaction. While people technically were not buying forgiveness of sins, it became associated with this in the minds of many. Priestly absolution forgave, but the sacrament was not complete until the work of satisfaction was accomplished. The whole scheme was ripe for abuse. The church quickly discovered that it could enhance its revenue by encouraging the sale of a document that promised entrance into heaven.

While Luther did not know it at the time, the indulgences that became available in the area near Wittenberg were the result of some result of some backroom dealings that would make the shadiest of hedge fund managers blush. The story—even beyond the specifics of the indulgence trade—also sheds more light on why many people were fed up the with church and eager for change.

In sixteenth-century Germany, bishops were often princes and princes were often bishops—the two roles overlapped in unsavory ways. In Luther's time, Pope Leo X was looking for ways to finance the building of St. Peter's Basilica in Rome. (If you have been to Rome and seen the finished product, then you know how breathtakingly beautiful—and therefore, enormously expensive—this endeavor turned out to be.) He discovered a rich prospect to help with the project, the Hohenzollern ruler Albrecht, who was already Archbishop of Magdeburg, but who also desired the bishopric of Mainz (both were regions in Germany). Why would someone want to be bishop of two places? The church was a large landowner and the one who oversees a diocese also controls the income derived from the land in taxes and tithes. Thus, pluralism (holding more than one church office at the same time) was common. And so was simony, the buying and selling of positions in the ecclesiastical hierarchy.

While Albrecht lacked the funds to obtain the title of bishop of Mainz, the church came to the rescue and allowed the sale of indulgences in his territory. The proceeds would enable him to purchase the office, and also, raise the money necessary to build St. Peter's. The entire deal was orchestrated by the Fuggers, a powerful banking family from the German city of Augsburg.

As noted earlier, Luther had no knowledge of this complicated scheme that was manipulated by the highest offices in Christendom. And the indulgence was not available in his community. But he did know that some of the people from his local congregation in Wittenberg were traveling a fairly short distance to purchase indulgences. What he heard made his skin crawl. According to a treatise written later in his life, Luther understood that a preacher by the name of John Tetzel was teaching the following things:

> That he (Tetzel) had such grace and power from the pope that even if someone seduced the holy Virgin Mary and made her conceive, he could forgive him, provided he placed the necessary sum in the box . . .
> Again, that if St. Peter were here now, he would not have greater grace or power than he (Tetzel) had . . .
> Again, if anyone put money in the box for a soul in purgatory, the soul would fly to heaven as soon as the coin clinked on the bottom.[3]

Luther was incensed at several levels. First, his understanding that God in Christ forgives sins because it is God's nature to be merciful was being challenged in a blatant way. Out of concern for a church that had betrayed its core conviction, Luther felt called to protest the sale of indulgences. *The Ninety-five Theses* was the result. Initially written in Latin and meant for debate among academics in the university, they were immediately translated into German and distributed throughout the land. The document included some sharp phrases designed to provoke argument:

3. See *Documents from the History of Lutheranism (1517–1750)*, ed. by Eric Lund (Minneapolis: Fortress Press, 2002), 13.

Those who believe that they can be certain of their salvation because they have indulgence letters will be eternally damned, together with their teachers. (Thesis 32)

Christians are to be taught that he who gives to the poor or lends to the needy does a better deed than he who buys indulgences. (Thesis 43)

The true treasure of the church is the most holy gospel of the glory and grace of God. (Thesis 62)[4]

While Luther believed his vocation was to issue a prophetic challenge to the church, he was also concerned for the care of souls in his local setting. In a teaching sermon from 1519, he lays out what the sacrament of penance really ought to look like. He deconstructs the parts of penance in a radical way. The traditional sequence of confession, absolution, and satisfaction is altered to become absolution, grace, and faith.[5] With regard to confession of sin, Luther recognizes its importance, and then, boldly declares that there is no such thing as an adequate confession of sins. Assurance does not come from having a "complete" confession, but rather, in knowing that your confession is never sufficient![6] This new idea about penance now places the word of forgiveness first. This word conveys the grace to the troubled conscience that enables it to trust Christ's promise or come to faith. All mention of making a complete confession or doing works of satisfaction have been set aside.

To no one's surprise, this drastic revision of penance unleashed a firestorm of response. And in what can only be described as a heroic stance, Luther the German Hercules refused to back down. But the drama of Luther the bold reformer squaring off against pope and emperor should not obscure a central concern on the level of the local

4. Martin Luther, "Ninety-five Theses" (1517), *LW* 31:28–31.
5. Luther, "Penance," *LW* 35:11.
6. Ibid., 15.

congregation. Luther's vocation as a preacher in the church in Wittenberg meant he came into contact with parishioners who spent hard-earned money on indulgences. They believed this document procured for them the forgiveness of sins. The sacrament of penance, instead of consoling troubled consciences, had become a big source of revenue for the church. People actually believed that God's forgiveness could, in part, be purchased. As a preacher, Luther insisted that the Word of God on forgiveness is clear: divine mercy cannot be merited nor is it for sale. While Luther certainly challenged the theology behind the selling of indulgences, it was his personal experience as a pastor that served as the catalyst for his work in the larger public realm. Seeing his people attempt to purchase forgiveness pushed him into the larger spotlight. The posting of the theses was never simply an academic matter. The one who hammered the document on the Wittenberg door was motivated by an intense concern for the souls of his people.

By 1520, almost three years after the posting of the theses, the church had run out of patience with Luther and his insistence on faith alone as that which determines a proper relationship with God. In June of that year, he was threatened with excommunication. A papal bull (or authentic letter from the pope) was published that described Luther as a beast bent on destruction. The document is making an appeal to Christ himself, who sits at the right hand of God in heaven:

> Foxes have arisen and have attempted to ruin the vineyard (Song of Solomon 2:15), whose wine-press you alone have trodden (Isaiah 63:3). When you ascended to your Father in heaven, you commended the care, management, and administration of the vineyard to Peter as its head and as your representative and also to his successors, as the church triumphant. A *wild boar of the woods* (italics mine) has attempted to destroy this vineyard.[7]

When Luther refused to take back his teaching a year later, the Edict of Worms lays out the consequences in plain language for anyone who comes to his aid:

> We strictly order . . . you shall refuse to give the aforementioned Martin Luther lodging, food, or drink, or offer him any help, support or assistance, by word or deed. . . . Wherever you might happen to meet him, you shall take him prisoner, if you have sufficient force, and deliver him to us. . . . You shall receive suitable compensation for such holy work and for your effort and expense. . . .[8]

Was he a German Hercules or a wild boar? Whatever image is chosen, it is clear that Luther's vocation in the church led him to push against conventional boundaries in dramatic fashion. Less well-known is his calling as a preacher in his local congregation in Wittenberg. It is to this work we now turn.

To Confront and Comfort

The Reformation gave new attention to the pulpit.[9] While preaching was not wholly neglected in the late Middle Ages, there was a tendency to focus on the Lord's Supper at the expense of the sermon. Luther's Word-centered theology meant that the calling to preach now received a prominent role in worship. Luther's own vocation as a preacher occupied an enormous amount of his time. He took regular turns in the pulpit during his lengthy time in Wittenberg—which covers the last thirty-five years of his life. We have over 2,300 of his sermons. In 1528 alone, he preached 195 times over a 145-day period![10]

By many accounts, Luther was a fine preacher.[11] His sermons

---

7. Lund, *Documents*, 27.
8. Ibid., 33.
9. Kolb, *Confessor*, 86–87.
10. Bainton, *Here I Stand*, 273.

contain lively images drawn from daily life as he seeks to imbed God's Word in the lives of his listeners. I have before me in my office a print of a famous painting of the Reformation done by the artist Lucas Cranach. The original is on an altar in Wittenberg in the very church where Luther proclaimed many of his sermons. It shows the reformer preaching to his congregation. He is in the pulpit with one hand resting on the Bible while the other points to Christ crucified, who is poised in mid-air between Luther and the congregation. The listeners of the sermon are enraptured by the words of the preacher. They gaze attentively at Jesus, but they are also clearly looking at Luther as well. Cranach's painting obviously has a teaching purpose: the sermon should point to the crucified Christ. And another lesson is also clear: the role model of the ideal preacher is Martin Luther, whose preaching captured the hearts and minds of his parishioners.

Doubtless, the image is correct in many respects. Luther's preaching was bracing and bold. Even though we have only words on a printed page, one can sense the life and energy that emanated from him as he challenged and comforted his listeners. And Luther was a fearless preacher. While, as we shall see, he could comfort his listeners with the sweet gospel, he was also an intrepid proclaimer of God's law. Note the sarcasm and anger that permeate a selection from a sermon preached in the main city church of Wittenberg in 1535. It should be remembered that Luther's congregation would have included many of the well-to-do of the city. The text is from Luke 16:19–31, the story of the rich man and the beggar Lazarus who lies ignored at his doorstep:

> (This text) . . . is addressed to the rich and arrogant people of

---

11. See Brecht II:57–59.

today. Unfortunately, as we know, such people most often think themselves pious and without greed. Vice has been turned into virtue. Greed nowadays has come to be viewed as talented, smart, careful stewardship . . . it (greed) is so dressed up and polished as no longer to be denominated as such. Neither prince nor peasant, nobleman nor average citizen is any longer considered greedy, but only upstanding . . . the common consensus being that the man who prudently provides for himself is a resourceful person who knows how to take care of himself. . . . The same holds true for other sins: pride is no longer pride, or sin, but honor. The proud man is no longer deemed arrogant but honorable, a commanding person, worthy of respect, a credit to his generation. . . . Thus there are no longer any sinners in the world, but—God have mercy!—the world is full of holy people.[12]

The relevance of Luther's words to our own situation is so obvious that little comment is needed. Our consumer society puts a high premium on appearances. All around us, there is evidence of a "wretched excess" that seeks to justify its prodigal ways by suggesting that it is simply the well-deserved fruit of hard work. This might also be a preview of "Psychological man," born to be pleased (see Chapter four). He has little place for sin in his worldview. Enclosed within himself, the possibility of being accountable in any significant way to a higher power fails to make sense.

But above all, Luther was known for his ability to preach the gospel or the "good news" that we are loved by God in Christ in spite of our unworthiness. All this is accomplished in the "great exchange," whereby Jesus takes upon himself our sin and rebellion and gives to us in return his forgiveness, wholeness, and righteousness. In a sermon on the Resurrection, Luther uses the dramatic language of battle to convey to his listeners what Christ has done for them. Notice

12. Martin Luther, "Sermon for First Sunday after Trinity" (1535) as found in *Faith and Freedom. An Invitation to the Writings of Martin Luther*, ed. by John F. Thornton and Susan B. Varenne (New York: Vintage, 2002), 169.

135

how personal the language is for Luther. He does not talk about sin in "general," but rather, about his own sin and, correspondingly, his own Christ:

> . . . for if I look at my sins, they will destroy me. Therefore I must look to Christ, who has taken my sins upon himself, crushed the head of the serpent, and become the blessing. Now they no longer burden my conscience, but rest upon Christ, whom they desire to destroy. Let's see how they treat him. They hurl him to the ground and kill him! O God . . . where is now my Christ and my Savior? But then God appears, delivers Christ, and makes him alive. . . . What now has become of sin? There it lies under his feet. If I then cling to this, I have a cheerful conscience like Christ, because I am without sin. Now I can defy death, the devil, and sin to do me any harm.[13]

This is only a glimpse of the power of Luther's preaching and the printed word hardly does justice to the underlying power of the message. But in his vocation as preacher, he accomplishes (along with his many colleagues) a paradigm shift. He boldly confronts a church sunk in a mire of self-righteousness and renews it with a message about a God who comes not for the holy, but rather, the "ungodly" (Rom. 5:5).

Luther as preacher. Courtesy of Wikimedia Commons.

13. Ibid., 157.

Unthankful Beasts

Finally, one more piece must be added to this picture of Luther's calling in the church. It does not receive much attention, but it belongs to an honest appraisal of his vocation. Luther, for all his bold speech as a preacher who confronts and challenges his church, was often frustrated in this calling. This should not surprise. Those called to be prophets [to God's people often saw their message rejected. Think, among the many examples, of Moses smashing the Ten Commandments in disgust at the feet of the people of Israel as they worshipped a golden calf (Exodus 32). Or recall Jeremiah, known as the "weeping prophet," who laments his calling to a seemingly deaf people by uttering the following question: "Why did I come forth from the womb to see toil and sorrow, and spend my days in shame" (Jer. 20:18).

In 1529, Luther was angry at the way Christian liberty was being misunderstood and abused. He frankly told his people that he had no desire "to be the shepherd of such pigs." During Advent in the same year, he had reached the end of the line. Despite his admonitions, the people kept sinning more and more. For most of the first three months of 1530, he more or less stopped preaching, despite the pleas of colleagues and his prince to keep at it.[14]

What were the main sources of his frustration? Luther appears particularly frustrated at the congregation in Wittenberg's unwillingness to support the church. This was not a reference to his own pay as he received a salary directly from his prince because of his employment in the university. But he was astonished at the people's lack of support for the

---

14. Brecht II:288.

rest of the clergy, the schoolteachers, and the poor. Excerpts from a sermon in 1528 demonstrate the bite in Luther's words:

> This week we are asking for an offering. I hear that the people will not give the collectors anything and turn them away. Thanks be to God, that you unthankful people are so stingy with contributions and give nothing, but with foul words chase away the deacons . . . you absolutely unthankful beasts, unworthy of the gospel; if you do not repent I will stop preaching to you.[15]

As noted earlier, Luther was a fine preacher. But the seed often fell on stony ground in Wittenberg. His vocation as a preacher knew many moments of exasperation and frustration. The trajectory of the Lutheran Reformation was never a line ascending to higher and higher heights of glory. It was, rather, a message of grace for sinners and many of Luther's listeners remained stiff-necked and hard-hearted.

What does this mean?

Let me begin this section with a story that can be used to illustrate what it means to have a vocation in a congregation. I was working in a community center in a poor neighborhood while going to seminary. The region was a mix of black, Puerto Rican, and Italian families. There were at least three Catholic churches within a six-block radius of where I worked. One morning, I was walking in the area with a group of teenagers when one of them announced, "Father Hernandez is coming down the street." A remarkable transformation took place before my eyes. Shirts were tucked in, shoes tied, and hair tidied. No more shuffle as backs were straightened. To my amazement, as the priest passed, my charges actually lined the sidewalk so he could proceed as if in a parade. A collection of

---

15. Ibid., 289.

greetings came his way, but the collared and imperial Father Hernandez made no eye contact. He mumbled a good morning and strolled through the group, impersonal and aloof.

In Luther's time, the church was clearly a danger to vocation, or we might say, it caused the community to lose its sense of vocation. This is true in our day as well. Father Hernandez can stand for a church that relegates a sense of calling to the clergy. When this happens, the laity are also not equipped to go into the world where their service is needed. This can occur in several ways.

The church is a danger to vocation when it gets identified with clergy, authority structures, buildings, and sacred spaces. We necessarily set apart pastors to preach the gospel and administer the sacraments. And it is important to respect the pastoral office. But this very act of "setting apart" can frustrate a sense of calling among the laity because of the temptation to think that clergy are somehow special or different from others in the church. We develop "Father Hernandez syndromes." (And let's be clear: this is hardly limited to Roman Catholicism!) The thinking goes something like this: church leaders are trained to preach and teach the Bible. They handle "holy things" in baptism and the Lord's Supper. Maybe they are closer to God as well? Perhaps they are the ones who truly have callings.

Let us be careful to note that this is not only an issue for community members. Far too many clergy and church leaders also embrace this syndrome. Often, this is done in a subtle way. Pastors and church leaders monopolize the time of regular members by overloading them with so-called "church work." Stewardship talk is inordinately focused on what happens within the community by its stress on the importance of giving to the congregation. Moreover, the vast majority of preaching and teaching neglects to talk about what it means to be called to be citizen, a parent, or a spouse. The overall effect is to confine "holiness" within the boundaries to the Christian community when the whole purpose is to equip people for their callings in the world.

Furthermore, there is the issue of sacred space. Many of our buildings are designed, as they should be, to create a sense of the holy when you enter them. Sometimes, there are stained glass windows. There might be an elevated altar or pulpit. The overall effect is solemn. Often, we are enticed into thinking that whatever happens in the building is deeply connected with God while the outside world is something lesser. Reading Scripture on Sunday mornings or assisting with communion is linked with having a "real" calling.

One irony here is that the two major figures of the Judeo-Christian tradition, Moses and Jesus, received their own calling far from any "holy" place. Exod. 3:1–6 reminds us that Moses, a fugitive from justice (wanted for murder), heard God's voice in the midst of the burning bush while tending to his sheep. Jesus, too, was in the wilderness at the Jordan River when he saw the heavens ripped open and heard that he was the beloved Son with whom God was pleased (Mark 1:9–11).

At the same time, the community is absolutely essential for vocation. This may not entail an actual building, of course. But it will mean some sort of gathering where a pastoral leader proclaims the promise. As I have tried to stress in this work, a Christian sense of calling has to be undergirded by Christ. Vocation is deeply grounded in baptism. Life is a pattern of dying and rising with Christ. God's Word both challenges our tendency toward self-worship and frees us to live in the present, fully alive to the needs of the neighbor and community. A life that is not nourished by God's Word as it is proclaimed from the pulpit, font, and altar risks becoming emaciated and turned in on itself.

Furthermore, the Christian community plays a vital role in the cultivation of a sense of calling. If vocation is finally all about serving the neighbor, then the church can be a crucial place for learning about the needs of those around me and throughout the world. It is in our common life together that I hear about the need for childcare for the single mom with cancer, the elderly man's lawn who needs mowing, the struggle of urban kids often written off as "lost," and the victims of an earthquake in China. Crucial for vocation is tending to the needs of the overlooked and marginalized. The community can or should be the place where the invisible become visible.

In summary, to ask again the question at the head of this section: what does all this mean? What is the relationship between vocation and the Christian community? Luther's experience is instructive for us. He certainly did not idolize the church. When it was in error, as happened in the indulgence controversy, he confronted it boldly and noisily. And when he turned his attention to the underlying theology and the false notion that we can earn our merit God's favor, he spared no one—especially the hierarchy he thought should have known better. But it was never Luther's intention to leave the church and found a separate community. He was thrown out in spite of his attempts at reform. Also, Luther's criticism should not obscure his essential love for the church—especially when it was understood as the place where the unlovable heard and experienced the remarkable news that they were loved.

So, on one level, we should expect a lot of the church. Because it is essential for a robust sense of vocation, we ought to demand that it be a place where God's promise is proclaimed boldly, clearly, and imaginatively in preaching, baptism, and the Lord's Supper. The church also ought to be a place where our idols are called into question. Too many Christians prefer to isolate themselves from the real problems of the world. We hunker down in our easy chairs, the television remote close at hand, while ignoring the plight of the poor, the hungry, and the outcasts.

But in another way we should also be prepared for frustration. Luther's own congregation was composed of "unthankful beasts." This should not have surprised him or us. God's people are not only saints in Christ, but they are sinners as well. That means they will often be slow to change, alarming in their greed, and often, overflowing with self-regard. And we would do well to recognize that we fit in well with such a crowd.

Questions for Discussion

1. Luther's calling led him to "bold speech" in the name of Christ crucified. How does "bold speech" happen in your congregation, if at all? How might you encourage such bold speech?

2. How does your own faith community promote a sense of vocation? What could be done to strengthen a sense of calling among the people?

8

———

Called to Work

If you are a manual laborer, you find that the Bible has been put into your workshop, into your hand, into your heart. It teaches and preaches how you should treat your neighbor. Just look at your tools—at your needle or thimble, your beer barrel, your goods, your scales or yardsticks or measure—and you will read this statement inscribed on them. Everywhere you look, it stares at you. Nothing that you handle every day is so tiny that it does not continually tell you this, if you will only listen. Indeed, there is no shortage of preaching. You have as many preachers as you have transactions, goods, tools, and other equipment in your house and home. All this is continually crying out to you: "Friend, use me in your relations with your neighbor just as your would want your neighbor to use his property in his relations with you."[1]

As mentioned in the introduction, in our age, the understanding of vocation has often been restricted to the world of work. If the word "vocation" enters the modern

1. Martin Luther, "Commentary on the Sermon on the Mount," (1532), *LW* 21:37.

vocabulary, then it is often conflated with "vocational" and the learning of a specific trade in plumbing, electronics, or carpentry, and so on. We have tried in this study to say otherwise. Our previous chapters have been devoted to the wide number of callings we have been given by God, including home and family, citizenship, and the church. But now, we finally turn to the arena of daily labor and look at the work to which Luther was called in his life. As was the case in the other areas we examined, there is a wealth of material from Luther's story that could be used in a chapter like this. To make the task more manageable, we will restrict ourselves to Luther's vocation as a scholar and teacher. We will see how that calling developed in the monastery, and then, we will focus on how it was exercised in the crucible of his enforced stay of nine months in the Wartburg Castle. Finally, we will examine Luther as a teacher—how his students saw him and his relationship to them.

"It Will Be the Death of Me . . ."

When Luther entered the monastery in Erfurt in 1505, he also embarked on a path that would lead to a doctoral degree in theology. This didn't happen at first. During his early years, he was preparing himself to be an Augustinian monk and priest. But by 1507, he was on an academic track that would lead to his appointment as a professor of theology at the University of Wittenberg in 1512.

Given the volume of Luther's writings and his fame as a preacher and teacher, many have assumed that his calling as a professor came naturally to him. But nothing could be further from the truth. When the head of his monastic order, Johann von Staupitz, who was also his spiritual advisor and mentor, told Luther that he was being appointed as a doctor of theology in Wittenberg, the future reformer was appalled. He offered up at least fifteen objections, concluding with the exclamation that such a position would "be the death of me." Staupitz countered with a jest designed to take the edge off Luther's fears: "Are you not aware that our Lord God has much more important business to conduct? For these things he needs wise counselors up in heaven as well." In other words, however things turned out, God would put Luther to use—even if it meant dying and joining him in heaven![2]

Later on, Luther would be grateful he had received Staupitz's command to teach. It comforted him to know that he was not a professor and teacher because of his own self-assessment. Rather, the church appointed him: "I, Doctor Martin Luther, have been called and forced to take the doctor's degree. This was against my own thinking and I did it only out of obedience. I was compelled to occupy the chair in theology at the university and I swore on the Holy Scriptures to teach the Word of God truly and clearly."[3]

Luther was quickly swept up into the academic swirl. In 1516, the year before the explosion caused by the 95 Theses, he writes to a friend in a manner that gives us good insight into his breathless schedule:

> I need nearly two copyists or secretaries. All day long I do almost nothing else than write letters. . . . I am a preacher in the monastery, I am a reader during mealtimes, I am asked daily to preach in the city church . . . I am caretaker of the fish pond at Leitzkau . . . I lecture on Paul, and I am assembling [material for] a commentary on the Psalms. . . . See what a lazy man I am![4]

---

2. See James Kittelson, *Luther the Reformer* (Minneapolis: Augsburg, 1986), 83.

3. Martin Luther, "Glosse auf das vermeinte kaiserliche Edict," (1531), WA 30(3):386. My translation.

4. Martin Luther, "Letter to John Lang" (October 26, 1516), LW 48:27–28.

In the five years following the receipt of his doctorate degree, he lectured on the Psalms, Romans, Galatians, and Hebrews. But this was just the beginning of his prodigious output. By the time he would take his final breath in Eisleben in 1546, his writings would fill 120 volumes. Sometimes, he wrote in response to a particular situation. But his writings also reflect the efforts of the professor in the classroom. He lectured regularly on the Bible throughout his calling as a professor in Wittenberg. Over two-thirds of this labor is on the Old Testament. But perhaps the best way to study Luther at work is to view him in a situation where he had literally nothing else to do.

I Shall Not Be Silent

As we saw earlier, after his bold testimony before the Diet of Worms in 1521, Luther left the gathering, fearing he would soon die the death of a heretic. But there were other plans made for a "cooling off" period while his prince and other authorities decided what to do with him. On his way back from Worms, he was "kidnapped" and taken to the Wartburg, one of Frederick the Wise's castles near the city of Eisenach. He was virtually alone in the huge fortress, save for a few attendants. But he was not quiet. For the next nine months, a torrent of letters, treatises, sermons as well as a magnificent translation poured forth from Luther's pen. As he warned the Archbishop of Mainz in the midst of confinement: "I shall not be silent."[5] Luther's time at the Wartburg affords a fine opportunity to see him in his calling as a scholar as he makes a determined attempt to "get the Word out."

As might be imagined, the first days in the Wartburg were

5. Ibid., 343.

bewildering. He had been forcibly removed from a turbulent arena of action. He went from testifying before emperors, princes, and bishops at Worms to a lonely room stuck high in the tower of a massive fortress. His initial weeks were marked by poor health (chronic constipation) and a restlessness (he reported he was "drunk with leisure") that must have unnerved him.[6]

But before long, Luther finds his stride and begins putting his significant scholarly gifts to work. He writes treatises on the sacrament of confession and the question of monastic vows. He authors a commentary on the Magnificat, the humble song of Mary when she hears she has been chosen to give birth to Jesus (Luke 1:46–55). But above all, Luther wants to make sure the German people are able to hear and read the gospel for themselves. From his prison, he issues forth two jewels that will shine brightly for generations: his postils or sermons on the Advent and Christmas biblical texts and his majestic translation of the New Testament.

We have already looked at Luther's vocation as a preacher in the chapter on his calling in the church, so we will not focus on the sermons. But worthy of attention is a small essay he wrote at the Wartburg that was attached to his book of sermons. Called *A Brief Instruction on What to Look for and Expect in the Gospels*, it highlights the theology behind his labors as a translator. In this essay, Luther makes clear that the Bible is God's Word, and as a communication from God, it needs to be listened to carefully. But the problem in his day is a singular focus on seeing Jesus simply as an example to be followed. This misses the point of the New Testament and turns Christ into a "Moses" or lawgiver. Rather, stresses Luther, the central content of the gospels is the Gospel or the good news that God

6. Ibid., 225.

in Christ has made us his own. As he puts it, "The chief article and foundation of the gospel is that before you take Christ as an example, you accept and recognize him as a gift, as a present that God has given you and that is your own."[7] Once you have grasped what Christ has done for you, then it is fine to turn to him as an example. But to focus only on the latter is to "remain as pagan as ever."[8]

What is Luther saying here? His work as a translator is devoted to making the reader of the Bible encounter the living Christ in the text. He knows that a lifeless translation of these pages would be highly ironic. The entire goal of Scripture is to arrest, convict, and console the reader. The object is not merely historical knowledge, but something much higher. A good translation conveys through these words the great fire of love that God has for us, which then leads our hearts and consciences to be happy, secure, and content.

With this framework in mind, Luther puts his considerable language skills to work. In the space of eleven weeks, he takes the Greek and Latin texts he learned as a student and monk and turns them into a German New Testament. While not the first translation into German, it far surpassed anything that had been done up to that time. The job was so well done that Luther's translation continues to be read up to our own day. Its heavy use down through the centuries means it will also play an important role in shaping the German language itself.

The pace of the work itself in the Wartburg was feverish. And the final product did not come easy. In fact, he would continue to revise the translation for the rest of his life. In the midst of this project, he stated, "I have undertaken the

---

7. Martin Luther, "A Brief Instruction on What to Look for and What to Expect in the Gospels" (1521), LW 35:119.
8. Ibid., 117.

task of translating the Bible (into German). This was necessary for me to do; otherwise I might have died thinking I was a learned man."[9] Moreover, consistent with his desire that the living voice of Christ be amplified in the text, he even took certain liberties with his translation. The most famous example is found in Romans and Paul's description of the believer in Christ as being "justified by faith apart from works of the law" (Rom. 3:28). Luther adds the word "alone" after the phrase "justified by faith" even though it is lacking in the original Greek. Because he believed translation should not be literal or wooden, but rather, faithful to the original sense of the text, Luther argued the "alone" was needed to bring out Paul's meaning in German.[10]

The New Testament translation came out in 1522, shortly after Luther left the Wartburg and returned to Wittenberg to provide guidance to the emerging movement of reform. The printers' first run of 5,000 copies sold out immediately. The entire Bible would be translated by 1534. Because Luther was not as learned in Hebrew, the original language of the Old Testament, it took a team of Wittenberg theologians to produce this text. Luther never received a cent for his work in royalties. This would be true of his other writings as well.

9. Martin Luther, "Ein Missive an Hartmut von Kronberg" (1522), WA 10(2):60. Translation mine.
10. Martin Luther, "On Translating: An Open Letter" (1530), LW 35:188–89.

Luther's German Bible. Courtesy of Wikimedia Commons.

Luther spent nine months in his fortress of exile. He worried about his health and had trouble sleeping. He struggled with the loneliness that accompanied his isolated location. But, above all, his time in the Wartburg reveals his deep sense of call as a scholar and theologian. Over a decade earlier, Johann Staupitz recognized Luther's gifts and pushed him into an academic vocation. Luther, in turn, labored hard in God's vineyard, but he was never overly impressed with the result. Toward the latter part of his life, he wrote the following:

> If, however, you feel and are inclined to think you have made it, flattering yourself with your own little books, teaching or writing, because you have done it beautifully and preached excellently; if you are highly pleased when someone praises you in the presence of others; if you perhaps look for praise, and would sulk or quit what your are doing if you did not get it—if you are of that stripe, dear friend, then take yourself by the ears, and if you do this in the right way you will find a beautiful pair of big, long, shaggy, donkey ears. Then do not spare any

expense! Decorate them with golden bells, so that people will be able to hear you wherever you go, point their fingers at you, an say, "See, See! There goes that clever beast, who can write such exquisite books and preach so remarkable well." That very moment you will be blessed and blessed beyond measure in the kingdom of heaven. Yes, in that heaven where hellfire is ready for the devil and his angels.[11]

The Professor and His Students

Our focus on Luther's vocation as a scholar would not be complete without a glance at his actual work as a professor in the classroom as well as his interaction with his students. As we have seen, in the years 1517–21, Luther became a famous figure in Europe. Naturally, this notoriety had repercussions for the Luther's school, the University of Wittenberg. In the early 1520s, students flocked to the town, doubling the size of the city and swelling the population of the school to the breaking point. Luther himself often spoke to over four hundred students in his lectures. These record enrollments would decrease because of concerns about the plague and the disturbances of the peasants' rebellion. But Wittenberg's student body did rebound near the end of Luther's life. Overall, his presence was, undoubtedly, a boon for this young university (founded in 1502), located in a backwater of the Holy Roman Empire.

Besides his popularity, what was Luther like in the classroom? This is somewhat difficult to know for sure. We have one description from a George Benedict, who describes him sometime during the period from 1518–22:

He was a man of middle stature, with a voice which combined sharpness and softness: it was soft in tone, sharp in enunciation

---

11. Martin Luther, "Preface to the Wittenberg Edition of Luther's German Writings" (1539), LW 34:287–88.

of syllables, words and sentences. He spoke neither too quickly not too slowly, but at an even pace, with hesitation, and very clearly, and in such fitting order that each part flowed naturally out of what went before . . . and so his lectures never contained anything that was not pithy and relevant. And to say something about the spirit of the man: if even the fiercest enemies of the Gospel had been among his hearers, they would have confessed from the force of what they heard, that they had witnessed, not a man, but a spirit, for he could not teach such amazing things from himself, but only from the influence of some good or evil spirit.[12]

He lectured in the academic language of the day, which was Latin. But he also sprinkled German into his presentations. While his preaching tended to focus on New Testament books, his classroom expositions were more likely to be devoted to the Old Testament. And he relied heavily on the Christian tradition to help explain biblical texts. Augustine was his favorite, but the lectures are seasoned with a wealth of references to the early church fathers and some of the medieval mystics.

In the quote above, Luther's student Benedict seems to stress the orderliness of his professor's lectures, but he was also known to go on digressions or be influenced by the schedule of the church year. For example, near the end of his life, he spent a good deal of his classroom time on the book of Genesis. But when he came to the story of Joseph (in Genesis 37–50), it happened to coincide with the Christmas season. So, Luther set Genesis aside for a time, and turned instead to the prophet Isaiah's prediction of the Messiah. He would later break off from Genesis during the Easter season to treat the theme of the suffering servant in Isaiah 53.[13]

---

12. As quoted in Gordon Rupp, *Luther's Progress to the Diet of Worms* (Chicago: Wilcox and Follett, 1951), 44.
13. Theodore G. Tappert, "The Professor of Theology," in *The Mature Luther* (Decorah, Iowa: Luther College Press, 1959), 44–45.

Also to be noted is Luther's deep care and concern for his students. We have many illustrations of this from letters the reformer sent to city councils, mayors, pastors, and so on, where he pleads for financial help for those striving for their degrees. In fact, over half of his correspondence with students involves the need for money to allow them to go to school.[14] An excellent example of Luther's benevolence toward his students is to be found in a note he sent in 1534 to Dorothy Jörger, a wealthy widow who had sent a large amount of money to be used for needy students. Luther reports to her on how the money is being spent:

> I myself did not know and would not have believed that in this little town and poor university there are so many godly and gifted students who live all year on bread and water, enduring frost and cold, in order that they might study the Holy Scriptures and the Word of God. Your charitable gifts have been a great boon and refreshment to them. I have distributed about half the money. . . . I have given more to Andrew than to the others; he received ten gulden and later another ten, while the others received two, three and four gulden. This was done with advice from good friends, and all are delighted and thankful.[15]

The details here are especially noteworthy. Luther may have lectured at times before large audiences, but he was also intimately involved in the daily finances of some of his students. In the letter above, he appears to be a professor and a financial aid counselor at the same time.

Luther's attentiveness could sometimes extend to the area of love and romance. He worried about rumors that the women of Wittenberg were chasing the male students with the hopes of getting engaged, and then, married. Some of these unions

14. See Lewis Spitz, "Luther's Social Concern for his Students," in *The Social History of the Reformation*, ed. by Lawrence P. Buck and Jonathan W. Zophy (Columbus: Ohio State University Press, 1972) 249–70.
15. Luther, *Spiritual Counsel*, 181.

apparently took place without the knowledge of parents and Luther ended up writing and even preaching about this situation.[16] He was also troubled by reports that students were making regular visits to a wooded area near Wittenberg that was known to be frequented by prostitutes.

Luther counseled students concerning a number of different ailments. Low spirits or melancholy afflicted many. He suggested that one set of brothers, Hieronymous and Matthias Weller, needed to be more social and directed them to the company of others, where they might sing, raise a glass, or play games, and thus, keep their troubles in perspective. And he told Conrad Cordatus to be careful about the tendency of the mind to magnify physical ailments:

> I thank God that your health is being restored. But I pray you curb your suspicion that your are assailed by who knows how many diseases. You know the proverb, "Imagination produces misfortunes." Therefore you ought to take the pains to divert rather than to entertain such notions. I too must do this. For our adversary, the devil, walks about, seeking not only to devour our souls but also to weaken our bodies . . . for he knows that our physical health depends in large measure on the thoughts of our minds.[17]

Finally, Luther was also aware that students often looked for excuses to avoid studying. While fears connected with an outbreak of the plague are certainly nothing to be minimized, Luther apparently felt that, in some cases, it became an excuse for avoiding academic work. In 1535, Luther wrote the following sardonic letter to his prince, John Frederick:

> Meanwhile I have observed that many of the young students have rejoiced over rumors of a pestilence, for some of them have developed sores from carrying their schoolbags, some have

---

16. Spitz, "Luther's Social Concern," 268.
17. Luther, *Spiritual Counsel*, 98–100.

acquired colic from their books, some have developed scabs on the fingers with which they write, some have picked up goutiness from their papers, and many have found their ink to be getting moldy. In addition, many have devoured letters from their mothers, and these have made them heartsick and homesick. There may well be more weaknesses of this kind than I know.[18]

Overall, Luther's vocation as a professor reveals him as one who came to his calling reluctantly, almost pushed into it by his mentor, Johann Staupitz. But he soon came to embrace his role as a teacher of the church. As we have seen, his experiences as a professor in Wittenberg reveal his passion to impart the gospel and sound learning to listeners. But he also became deeply involved in the lives of his students, advocating for them in time of need and cajoling them when sloth threatened.

Above all, his remarkable production of treatises and letters, to say nothing of his translation of the New Testament, while ensconced in the Wartburg is testimony to his deep desire that the people of God need to be deeply grounded in the Word. As he would comment in 1520 near the end of *The Freedom of a Christian*:

> Human nature and natural reason, as it is called, are inclined toward superstition and imagine that, when laws and works are prescribed, it must mean that righteousness can be obtained by following them. In addition, since this viewpoint is confirmed by the practice of all earthly lawgivers, it is impossible for them on their own to escape the slavery of works and comprehend the freedom of faith. Therefore, we need to pray that the Lord may mold or shape us as *theodidacti*, that is, those who are taught by God (John 6:5). In this way, God will write his law on our hearts, just as he promised to do.[19]

18. Ibid., 246.
19. Luther, *Freedom*, 95.

So, for Luther teaching was indeed a high calling. Whether his audience be the broader one of Christendom or a classroom in the fledgling University of Wittenberg, he believed that few offices provided a better opportunity to serve the needs of both church and society. As he said in 1530:

> I will simply say briefly that a diligent and upright schoolmaster or teacher, or anyone who faithfully trains and teaches boys, can never be adequately rewarded or repaid with any amount of money . . . If I could leave the preaching office and my other duties, or had to do so, there is no other office I would rather have than that of schoolmaster or teacher of boys; for I know that next to that of preaching, this is the best, greatest, and most useful office there is. Indeed, I scarcely know which one of the two is the better.[20]

What Does This Mean?

Luther had little doubt that God was at work in the world. God even used imperfect instruments such as the reformer himself to exhibit God's care for creation. As a translator, God was using Luther's significant intellectual and language skills to clarify the words of Scripture so that they might be clearly understood by the German people. As a teacher, God was using Luther to instruct his students about the nature of God's Word and how it related to their own lives. As a mentor, God was using Luther to care for the well-being of his students beyond the lectures of the classroom. Behind the work of translating, teaching, and mentoring was God's providential hand, caring for his creation much as an earthly mother or father might look after the needs of a family.

However, in our day, there is much confusion about how God works in the world and some of it is related to how we view

---

20. Martin Luther, "A Sermon on Keeping Children in School" (1530), *LW* 46:252–53.

our own work. As I stated in the introduction, the reigning belief among young people *in the church* is something called "moralistic, therapeutic deism."[21] That sounds like a mouthful, but it basically boils down to the belief that God will reward good people with heaven and send bad people to hell. Also, the main object of faith is to enable you to feel good about yourself. And finally, God is "out there" somewhere, but not very involved in daily life.

Just about every point of this perspective contradicts Luther's understanding of vocation. As we have seen, God's grace does not divide the world up into "good" and "bad" people. Rather, all have fallen short of God's glory and depend solely on God's mercy. Further, the point of religion is not to make you feel good about yourself. That turns faith into something that is basically self-serving. The point of religion is to love God (something enabled by God) and serve the neighbor. The view that God is simply indifferent and aloof from creation and human affairs is a vast distance from Luther's belief that God "daily and abundantly provides shoes and clothing, food and drink, house and farm, spouse and children, fields livestock, and all property—along with all the necessities and nourishment for this body and life."[22] And it certainly is in dramatic tension with the teaching that, in Christ, God has entered deeply into human flesh and human experience.

But just how is God active in the world? In our time, science (which has blessed us with so many discoveries) seems to reign supreme. Admittedly, it does feel like the world runs on its own without any help from an outside power or force. It is easy to

---

21. See Smith and Denton, *Soul Searching*, 118–71. It might be added that the young people were taught (or caught?) these beliefs by their parents, mentors, and churches.
22. Luther, "The Small Catechism," in *BC*:354.

explain things such as tides, illnesses, thunderstorms, and the change of seasons without talking about God. As some have suggested, nature appears to be "self-enclosed" and mention of God seems forced or even old-fashioned.

In response to God's apparent absence, some have tried to "save" him (how is that for irony—now we are saving God!) by saying that there is a place for God in events that seem extraordinary or beyond rational explanation. So, when stage four cancer inexplicably disappears, we put it down to an "act of God." Or when a child falls accidentally from a tenth floor balcony and miraculously survives, we point to divine intervention. This is an image of God that might be likened to a firefighter. God appears on the scene when things are desperate, and sometimes, makes an astonishing rescue. It is not that these views are wrong. I would certainly be thankful to God in the examples just mentioned. But a God who acts in such a way seems so limited and uninvolved. For most of life, God appears to be an idle spectator, content to watch while others play the game.

But the eyes of faith provide another perspective and this is where talk of vocation can make sense—especially in the world of work. My teacher Jim Nestingen liked to tell his students about the marvel in every loaf of bread. For most people, there is nothing extraordinary about the bread we buy in a grocery store. It seems so ordinary—wrapped, priced, and sitting on a shelf with forty other items that look just like it. But step back for a moment and think about what it took to bring the bread to your table. It started with seed that no one had made. This seed was planted in plot of good, black earth that came from no human hand. The right amount of rain and sun (again, not a human product) results in wheat. From there, it is harvested by a farmer and sent off to be milled, baked, and trucked to a store. Finally, it is sold to you and set out for dinner. Nestingen comments:

> As common as it might be, there is a miracle in every slice of bread—the miracle of fertile soil, of decent weather, of the hands of men and women, of water and yeast all coming together. Even if it's store-bought white bread containing as much air as flour, how could anyone ever pay for all the gift in it?[23]

God could have rained manna down from heaven, as God did with the ancient Israelites. Or God could mysteriously multiply existing stocks of loaves and fishes in order to feed people. But God uses our callings to tend to the needs of the world. Bread does not happen without the work of the farmer, miller, baker, and merchant. Luther says that people function as God's "masks" to accomplish God's will on earth. It is God at work in vocation. We are God's instruments. God is not absent, but *hidden* behind the various gift and talents of the laborers.[24]

Let me provide another example. My elderly mother died of a stroke. Her last three weeks were spent in hospice. While I prayed for her healing, I also knew it was unlikely that she would recover. But I was constantly amazed and grateful for the ways God cared for her during her last days through the vocations of the workers. She had a doctor who saw her faithfully and patiently answered our family's questions. She had a group of nurses who tended to her needs, and moreover, helped our family when we were sad, tired, or puzzled about the effects of strokes. She had a maintenance man who kept her room clean and who hummed gospel hymns as he went about his work. And this just scratches the surface, saying nothing about visits from pastors, relatives and friends. All of

---

23. James A. Nestingen, *Roots of our Faith* (Minneapolis: Augsburg Publishing House, 1979), 27.
24. See the excellent section in Wingren's *Luther on Vocation*, 137–43.

it was a manifestation of vocation—of God using people in their callings to serve a neighbor in need.

When we view the world through the eyes of vocation, it becomes difficult to talk about God's "absence." God is anything but distant and aloof. Nor is God a spectator, content to watch the action from afar. The lens of vocation provides a far different perspective, one that captures the spirit of Psalm 24:1: "The earth is the Lord's and all that is in it; the world and all that live in it."

Many object to this line of thinking about vocation and work. It sounds like work is being romanticized. What about those who are unemployed? What about people for whom work is demeaning or vastly undervalued? Couldn't this idea be used to justify people staying in their place (after all, it is a vocation), and thus, upholding an unjust status quo?

These hard questions cannot be dodged. A few things might be mentioned in reply. As for those who are unemployed, it is true that they suffer even more in a culture such as ours that tends to idolize work. We are often defined by our work. This is especially true for men, but becoming increasingly the case for women as well. Our identities are intertwined with what we do for a living. In other words, unemployment is closely linked with shame. The loss of a position does not just mean the absence of a regular paycheck or an extended period of enforced and unwelcome leisure. There is also the nagging suggestion that there is something wrong with *me*. It is not surprising that joblessness is followed by depression and anxiety.

There are no easy answers here, but it should be pointed out that Luther never conflated work with vocation. A person is always called, whether one has a job or not. This does not automatically ease the sting and even shame that comes with the loss of a paycheck, but it does point to a larger horizon where our identity comes from our union with Christ in baptism and not from our ability to live up to a cultural standard that equates status with employment and a certain level of income. The pastoral task for clergy and lay people is to remind the unemployed of this great truth without ignoring the genuine pain that comes from job loss. In addition, one would hope that the Christian community could supply the resources (or point to them) and friendship so important to those seeking work.

Vocation has also been challenged on another front. There has been a significant amount of healthy criticism about the use of vocation to justify an unjust status quo. Some have suggested that vocation is inherently hierarchical, and therefore, susceptible to exploitation. There is always the temptation for one possessing power in a relationship to use it in immoral ways. And when that power is undergirded with "vocation," the door is wide open for abuse. For example, in the world of work, a boss might perceive a sense of calling that causes him or to "lord" it over his employees. Such a person perceives their position as possessing a "divine blessing" that feeds a sense of superiority and entitlement. This leads to mistreatment of employees. The classic and most dramatic case is the slave master and the slave, but this same power dynamic is played out in lesser but numerous ways in workplaces everywhere.

There is little question that vocation has been used this way.[25] But as this book has attempted to stress repeatedly, the power dimension in any relationship should look different when a sense of calling is present. From a vocational perspective, grounded in the Christian faith, the one in power

25. See the excellent review in Schuurman, *Vocation*, 76–116.

stands under the authority of one who tells his followers that the first shall be last and the last first. A sense of calling has the possibility of transforming power from an ethic of domination to an ethic of service. So, while we must be mindful of the potential abuses of vocation, we must also take care to underline that a sense of calling always implies a *caller*. In the Christian faith, this Caller crosses lines, upends norms, and challenges the status quo. If vocation results in the perpetuation of injustice, then serious questions must be asked about how the ones with the power understand the crucified and risen God who has summoned them.[26]

Questions for Discussion

1. Luther clearly shaped many vocations by his teaching in the classroom. Who are the teachers in your life who did something similar for you and others?
2. Many people—even Christians—feel a sense of God's absence in the world. How does a robust sense of vocation challenge this view?
3. What do you think of the criticism that vocation can lead to power being used unjustly?

---

26. Deanna A. Thompson, *Crossing the Divide. Luther, Feminism, and the Cross* (Minneapolis: Fortress Press, 2004) is a clear and helpful discussion of Luther's theology of the cross as well as addressing the concerns of feminists about how this chief symbol of the Christian faith has been used to perpetuate injustice.

9

Conclusion

The Angelus by Millet. Courtesy of Wikimedia Commons.

Give us this day our daily bread.

What is this? Answer:

In fact, God gives daily bread without our prayer. Even to all evil people, but we ask in this prayer that God cause us to recognize what our daily bread is and to receive it with thanksgiving.

What then does "daily bread" mean? Answer:

Everything included in the necessities and nourishment for our bodies, such as food, drink, clothing, shoes, house, farm, fields, livestock, money, property, and upright spouse, upright children, upright members of the household, upright and faithful rulers, good government, good weather, peace, health decency, honor, good friends, faithful neighbors and the like.[1]

It has often been said that grace, or more precisely justification by grace through faith, and vocation are the twin pillars of the Lutheran reformation. There is little question that a Word of grace is sorely needed in this age. As is always the case, that Word needs to be communicated in new and fresh ways. Perhaps more than ever, the church needs preachers and teachers of great imagination. The competition for hearts and minds is fierce. There is a breathtaking array of images and voices vying for our attention. Some of the messages contain helpful information. Often, however, the idea being communicated suggests that we are not really complete unless we conform to a certain image, attain a specific income, or purchase a particular product. Moreover, there is such an inordinate amount of attention focused on our own needs, wants, and desires that the well-being of neighbors near and far tends to get moved far down our list of priorities.

Few figures in the history of church have spoken that Word

---

1. Martin Luther's explanation to the fourth article or part of the Lord's Prayer as found in his "Small Catechism" in BC:357.

of grace with more clarity than Martin Luther. Of course, Luther himself would claim that he is only echoing something first found in Scripture, especially in the writings of Paul. Perhaps the most compelling thing about Luther was his ability to cut through all the verbiage and say with clarity and boldness that God in Christ loves the unlovable. Period. No conditions or fine print or asterisks. It is a Word that unsettles (because it undermines our attempts at control). But finally, it is a Word that sets its listeners free. The sense of liberation soars far beyond anything available in this earthly life. And there are a lot of good things to be found in this world.

Luther got this right. But as this study makes clear, he also got some things wrong.[2] He was a child of his times in many ways. And he also spoke and said things that were wrong even by the standards of the sixteenth century. Unfortunately, if Luther gets attention in our time beyond the boundaries of the churches bearing his name, then it is usually because of the horrible and intemperate things he said about his opponents. Some are unable to look past these statements and that is understandable. But for those who do, they might find that same Word of grace that Luther himself found so captivating.

This book has also shown that this Word of grace is organically linked to vocation for Luther. It is not a Word that floats abstractly above the messiness of human life. Rather, it is a Word for this life. It is a Word meant to be lived—but not a love to be earned—in our numerous callings. Luther demonstrated this was the case as he described what this Word did to him as an individual. We also saw how it inevitably spilled over into his callings as a son, spouse, parent, citizen,

---

2. A fascinating critical but appreciative study of Luther's theology is Hans-Martin Barth's *The Theology of Martin Luther. A Critical Assessment* (Minneapolis: Fortress Press, 2013). Barth poses questions at the end of each chapter about the relevance of Luther's teaching for the church and world today.

pastor, and teacher. As the previous chapters have indicated, there is much to be mined in Luther's own life as we think about what it means to be faithful today.

Luther's teaching profoundly affected his world. There is little doubt that the towns and cities where the Reformation took hold where different places than before. Monasteries closed. Pastors married and had families. People no longer went on pilgrimages to view relics. The calendar was no longer crowded with holy days that honored a multitude of saints—something that brought smiles to merchants who were now free to peddle their goods instead of closing their shops. Bibles were more readily available and studied by a wider array of people. Preaching, teaching, and catechetical instruction shaped the hearts and minds of Christians in new ways. Doubtless, this picture is somewhat romanticized, but there is compelling evidence that Luther and the other reformers in his wake shook up their world in remarkable ways.[3]

But it also seems to be the case that the intervening centuries have been hard on the Reformation's understanding of vocation. The research here is so extensive that one hardly knows where to begin and a substantive discussion of this phenomenon is far beyond the borders we have set in this book.[4] The basic thrust of a very complicated history is that religion became a private matter, something isolated and separate from daily life. The forces of capitalism, driven by a

3. Steven E. Ozment, "The Reformation as Public Event," *Lutheran Theological Seminary Bulletin* 70 (1990), 1-15.
4. Max Weber's controversial but still relevant *The Protestant Ethic and the Spirit of Capitalism*, tr. Talcott Parsons (New York: Scribner's, 1958) was first published in 1905. It traces how the idea of vocation, once it is loosed from its theological moorings, allows for the untrammeled accumulation of wealth. Brad S. Gregory's *The Unintended Reformation. How a Religious Revolution Secularized Society* (Cambridge: Harvard University Press, 2012) is a brilliant summary of the many forces that combined to create the West's secular worldview. Unfortunately, he tends to repeat the old saw that Luther's theology, however unwittingly, was antinomian in its consequences.

consumer society, certainly applauded this change. Instead of having people governed by a sense of calling that yielded lives of restraint and moderation, the way was now free to exploit human desires in every imaginable dimension. Unshackled of faith, humans now become objects of sophisticated marketing machines designed to make all our wants into needs. Nor has the church been a victim or even an innocent bystander in these developments. It has often aided and abetted these changes by peddling a Christianity that is exclusively tepid, cushy, and oozing with solace. And in the meantime, the faith was gutted.

This book contains a modest suggestion that these developments are not inevitable. Perhaps, Christian communities, by looking back and recovering a vibrant tradition, can also move forward in a world that pushes God and faith to the boundaries (or merely the interior) of life.

So, at the conclusion of this study, let's end at the beginning. In other words, let's go back to the church basement and the congregational forum I spoke of in the introduction to this book. In the midst of their busy lives, those people came to church looking for a Word of grace. They wanted and needed to hear that they were forgiven and accepted in spite of their failures to love. They wanted to know that their lives had meaning and purpose in a culture that can make people feel small and insignificant. They surely did not need to know the nuances of Lutheran dogma (though that is fascinating to me) and my mistake was an overly long focus on those issues.

But maybe the real difficulty begins when they leave that church and enter a world that feels so secular. I know this from firsthand experience. I read Scripture in my daily devotions. I go to church and even have the opportunity to go to chapel regularly on the campus where I teach. My calling as a professor is, in part, to make the case for Christianity to students who often have little or no faith background. And yet, I am painfully aware of a gnawing sense of emptiness that seems to accompany life. The biblical story insists that a gracious God rules his creation. But other stories compete with that one for my attention. And they are often powerfully persuasive, including the one that suggests we are here, but for a brief time, and religion is merely a way we try to comfort ourselves in a cold and silent universe.

Thankfully, the Holy Spirit pulls me back from my lack of trust in God and into a faith where the space surrounding me is once again a "creation" into which I am called in love and service of neighbors near and far. Inextricably linked with this faith is the idea of vocation. This means that God is active in life, even the messy details, through the action of parents, spouses, citizens, and workers.

Our task is to equip people with the eyes to see God at work in their lives and in their world. God's great Word of grace and freedom is meant for the world. And people need help to think about ways to resist a culture that would prefer religion to either go away or be a private matter. As we have seen, Luther's own life gives us some pointers for how this might be done. But now the ball is in our court. How will we help people to nurture and maintain a sense of calling in their lives? What will be needed to not just send people forth from worship "into the world in service," but also shape minds and imaginations about the concrete meaning of that phrase without lapsing into a legalism that negates God's promises to us in our baptism?

The recovery of a sense of vocation will require a major transformation of what it means to be a Christian community. But as I Peter 2:9 reminds us, it is a renewal rooted in our actual identity: "But you are a chosen race, a royal priesthood, a holy nation, God's own people, in order that you may proclaim the mighty acts of him who called you out of darkness into his marvelous light." This Word, which has both challenge and promise in it, has carried Christians down through the centuries. May it, by God's will, bear us as well.

Index of Names

Partial Index of Subjects